United States Government Accountability Office

Report to Congressional Committees

July 2012

FOOD SAFETY

FDA's Food Advisory and Recall Process Needs Strengthening

July 2012

FOOD SAFETY

FDA's Food Advisory and Recall Process Needs Strengthening

Why GAO Did This Study

Numerous outbreaks of foodborne illnesses in past years continue to draw public attention to the safety of the nation's food supply. Prompt responses from government entities and the food industry can play a vital role in stopping the spread of illnesses and deaths, but unwarranted recalls of food products can trigger serious economic losses for the food industry. In response to congressional direction regarding the FDA Food Safety Modernization Act, GAO (1) examined government entities having the authority to order product recalls and how FDA implements its authority; (2) examined the challenges FDA faces, if any, in advising the public about food recalls or outbreaks of foodborne illness and how the agency has addressed these challenges; and (3) identified mechanisms that may compensate the food industry for erroneously ordered food recalls or erroneous food-related advisories. GAO reviewed documents from FDA and other government entities and FDA data and interviewed stakeholders from the food industry and consumer organizations, government officials, and experts in food safety or food law.

What GAO Recommends

GAO recommends, among other things, that FDA issue regulations or industry guidance to clarify its ordered food recall process and implement recommendations from others to address FDA communication challenges in advising the public about food recalls and outbreaks. The agency neither agreed nor disagreed with GAO's recommendations but cited ongoing agency actions that are to address most recommendations.

View GAO-12-589. For more information, contact Lisa Shames at (202) 512-3841 or shamesl@gao.gov.

What GAO Found

Several government entities, including federal agencies such as the Food and Drug Administration (FDA) and the Consumer Product Safety Commission, and some states such as Texas, have the authority to order product recalls. Generally, FDA is to follow the same process for implementing its food recall authority as other federal agencies use to order recalls of other products, including (1) determining that available evidence of a threat meets a standard of proof to order a recall, (2) offering a company the opportunity to voluntarily recall a product before a recall order is issued, and (3) providing the company with an opportunity to challenge a recall decision. FDA has internal procedures describing the steps it will take to order a food recall, although these procedures are not yet public and the agency has not issued regulations or industry guidance to clarify its ordered food recall process.

FDA faces a number of communication challenges when advising the public about food recalls or outbreaks of foodborne illness, ranging from balancing technical accuracy with timeliness of communications to coordinating messages with other agencies to meeting the needs of diverse public audiences. The agency has taken steps to begin meeting these challenges but has yet to fully address recommendations from GAO and others to fashion a comprehensive food recall communication policy and related implementation plans. Specifically, FDA has not (1) adopted a recommendation from its Advisory Committee on Risk Communication to create a policy for emerging events to more comprehensively address several of its communication challenges; (2) created plans recommended by the Institute of Medicine and National Research Council to help address coordination challenges surrounding its communications; or (3) fully implemented a recommendation from GAO's past work to determine jointly with the Department of Agriculture what, if any, additional approaches are needed for advising consumers about recalls. When GAO asked FDA officials how they had responded to these recommendations, they provided information on some actions they are taking. However, FDA's stated actions do not fully implement these recommendations. As a result of not implementing them, FDA may be missing opportunities to more comprehensively address its communications challenges.

Various government mechanisms—each with advantages and disadvantages described by individuals GAO interviewed—might be available to compensate food producers in case of an erroneously ordered food recall or erroneous food-related advisory, but GAO found no examples of such mechanisms that have been used to provide compensation. The mechanisms include a dedicated federal government program or federal government-subsidized insurance, among others. For example, individuals GAO interviewed said that a potential advantage of a dedicated program would be assurance to industry that a mechanism would be available, but a potential disadvantage may be that in lean budget times, funding for such a program may be difficult to obtain. Individuals GAO interviewed identified several factors that may come into play when deciding to establish any compensation mechanism, such as defining what constitutes an error or mitigating the potential for unintended consequences.

_____ United States Government Accountability Office

Contents

Figure

Abbreviations

AGR	Adjusted Gross Revenue
APHIS	Animal and Plant Health Inspection Service
CDC	Centers for Disease Control and Prevention
CORE	Coordinated Outbreak Response and Evaluation
FDA	Food and Drug Administration
FSMA	FDA Food Safety Modernization Act
HHS	Department of Health and Human Services
OMB	Office of Management and Budget
USDA	U.S. Department of Agriculture

United States Government Accountability Office
Washington, DC 20548

July 26, 2012

Congressional Committees

Numerous outbreaks of foodborne illnesses in past years continue to draw public attention to the safety of the nation's food supply. In the last several years, major outbreaks and product recalls have been associated with foods including peanut products, eggs, spinach, and cantaloupes. When such outbreaks are discovered, prompt responses from government and companies in the food distribution chain—the network of handlers, suppliers, and others involved in the production of food—can play a vital role in stopping the spread of illnesses and keeping the food supply safe; delays can result in more illnesses, as well as deaths. If unwarranted, however, advisories about adulterated or misbranded food products and recalls of those products can trigger serious economic losses for the food industry and discourage the consumption of healthful food, such as fresh produce. For example, in 2008, during an outbreak of illnesses caused by the bacterium *Salmonella*, the Department of Health and Human Services' (HHS) Food and Drug Administration (FDA) first warned consumers about certain tomatoes on the basis of information provided by other government agencies. Early in their work, government investigators used available evidence to associate the outbreak with raw tomatoes, but FDA's investigation subsequently implicated jalapeño and serrano peppers. Meanwhile, according to a tomato industry representative, tomato growers and shippers in several states lost an estimated $145 million in revenue.

Federal oversight of food safety has remained on our list of high-risk areas in need of broad-based transformation to achieve greater economy, efficiency, effectiveness, accountability, and sustainability since we added it in 2007,[1] largely because of fragmentation (i.e., 15 agencies collectively administering at least 30 laws) that has caused inconsistent oversight, ineffective coordination, and inefficient use of resources. FDA and the U.S. Department of Agriculture (USDA) have primary responsibility for the safety of the domestic and imported food supply. USDA is responsible for meat, poultry, processed egg products, and as soon as recently proposed

---

[1]See GAO, *High-Risk Series: An Update*, GAO-11-278 (Washington, D.C.: February 2011). See also GAO, *High-Risk Series: An Update*, GAO-07-310 (Washington, D.C.: January 2007).

regulations are finalized, catfish. Under the Federal Food, Drug, and Cosmetic Act, FDA is responsible for ensuring the safety of virtually all other food. FDA monitors recalls of food by industry and works with other agencies—including state and local governments, HHS's Centers for Disease Control and Prevention (CDC), and USDA—to identify and investigate multistate outbreaks of foodborne illnesses and alert the public to outbreaks.

In January 2011, the FDA Food Safety Modernization Act (FSMA) amended the Federal Food, Drug, and Cosmetic Act to give FDA authority to order the recall of food products other than infant formula, when a company fails to voluntarily recall the products.[2] Under FSMA, after FDA determines that there is a reasonable probability that a food product is adulterated under the Federal Food, Drug, and Cosmetic Act or misbranded with respect to labeling for major food allergens, and the use or exposure to that food will cause serious adverse health consequences or death to humans or animals, it must provide the company with the opportunity to voluntarily undertake a recall. Food is deemed to be adulterated under the Federal Food, Drug, and Cosmetic Act if, among other things, it bears or contains any poisonous or deleterious substance that may render it injurious to health. Until passage of this act, FDA could ask companies to voluntarily recall adulterated or misbranded food products, but it could not order them to do so, except for infant formula.

FSMA directed us to report on issues associated with FDA's new authority to order food recalls, as well as on the authority held by government entities to order recalls of other products. Accordingly, this report (1) examines key government entities having the authority to order product recalls and how FDA implements its authority; (2) examines the challenges FDA faces, if any, in advising the public about food recalls or outbreaks of foodborne illnesses and examines how FDA has addressed

---

[2]For purposes of this report, the term *recall* includes a firm's removal or correction of a marketed product. Corrections may include repair, modification, adjustment, relabeling, destruction, or inspection of a product without its physical removal to some other location. Similarly, the term *order* includes an agency's authority to directly mandate, require, or to make a determination that would require a recall under the law, or an agency's authority to obtain such an order through a court. Under the Federal Food, Drug, and Cosmetic Act, food includes both human and animal food, and the provisions of FSMA authorizing FDA to order food recalls apply to both human and animal food. This report, however, discusses only human food. Before January 2011, FDA had authority to order recalls for medical devices, radiation-emitting electronic products, biological products, tobacco products, and infant formula but not foods other than infant formula.

these challenges; and (3) identifies mechanisms that may compensate the food industry for erroneously ordered food recalls or erroneous food-related advisories, including the advantages and disadvantages of each.

To address these objectives, we reviewed information from the Congressional Research Service, the National Academies, and our own past work, as well as from academic sources and industry publications. We gathered documentation and met with officials from FDA, CDC, the Consumer Product Safety Commission, the Environmental Protection Agency, the Department of Transportation's National Highway Traffic Safety Administration, the Department of State, and USDA. We also gathered documentation from and met with representatives of the food industry, consumer organizations, and others to understand issues surrounding recalls and food-related advisories. To address our first objective, we identified key government entities with the authority to order product recalls by reviewing our prior work in this area, collecting legal documentation, interviewing agency officials, and working with the Association of Food and Drug Officials to contact their member states via e-mail. We examined how FDA implements its authority to order food recalls (other than infant formula) by reviewing FSMA and interim internal procedures from FDA. We also reviewed statutes, regulations, and guidance on ordered recalls of other products from FDA and the other federal agencies we identified. We also collected data from FDA on the number of ordered recalls and assessed the reliability of those data by reviewing documentation on the agency's data systems and interviewing FDA officials and found that the data were not reliable for our reporting purposes, which we discuss further in the report. To address our second objective, we reviewed documents from FDA and the National Academy of Sciences, among others. We also interviewed FDA officials, representatives of consumer and industry organizations, government officials from other state and federal agencies, and experts in food safety. To address our third objective, we reviewed the relevant literature and interviewed officials from international government entities such as the European Union. We also conducted semistructured interviews with representatives of consumer groups and industry organizations, officials from federal or state government, and experts in food safety or food law. We chose these interview respondents to reflect a range of perspectives. For further information on our scope and methodology, see appendix I.

We conducted this performance audit from May 2011 to July 2012 in accordance with generally accepted government auditing standards. Those standards require that we plan and perform the audit to obtain sufficient, appropriate evidence to provide a reasonable basis for our findings and conclusions based on our audit objectives. We believe that the evidence obtained provides a reasonable basis for our findings and conclusions based on our audit objectives.

Background

In addition to harming human health, outbreaks of foodborne illness can have serious economic consequences and undermine consumer confidence in the safety of the nation's food supply. In the past several years, consumers in the United States and abroad have experienced several noteworthy outbreaks of foodborne illness, including the following:

- *A 2011 outbreak of* Listeria monocytogenes *bacteria associated with cantaloupes grown in Colorado.* During this outbreak, CDC reported a total of 146 cases in 28 states, including 30 deaths and one miscarriage. According to a USDA document, this event was the largest outbreak of *Listeria* since a 1985 outbreak linked to a Mexican-style soft cheese which, according to HHS, resulted in 28 deaths and 20 miscarriages. The long-term economic effects to industry are not yet known, but USDA reported in November 2011 that prices for cantaloupe dropped about 34 percent in the wake of the outbreak.

- A 2011 *outbreak of* E. coli *O104:H4 bacteria in Germany and France, associated first with cucumbers, lettuce, and tomatoes but later traced to sprouts grown from fenugreek seeds exported by an Egyptian company.* During this outbreak, Germany's Robert Koch Institute reported 3,842 cases and 53 deaths. According to a European Union press document, farmers lost more than €227 million from May 26 through the end of June 2011. On the basis of requests for compensation from European Union member states, €227 million was expected to cover 50 percent (or 70 percent in some cases) of the usual producer price of cucumbers, tomatoes, lettuce, zucchini, and sweet peppers withdrawn from the market from May 26 through June 30, 2011.

- A 2010 *outbreak of* Salmonella Enteritidis *bacteria associated with shell eggs from Iowa.* CDC estimates that adulterated eggs caused 1,939 illnesses, and FDA reported that the outbreak prompted a nationwide recall of more than 500 million eggs packaged under several brand names. According to congressional testimony from an FDA official, this was the largest reported outbreak of *Salmonella* Enteritidis since the agency's outbreak surveillance started in the early 1970s. According to industry estimates, the generic shell-egg industry lost about $100 million in the month after the recall was announced, although prices returned within a few months to levels before the recall.

- A 2008-2009 *outbreak of* Salmonella *Typhimurium associated with peanut products from the Peanut Corporation of America*, resulting in a recall of products made at its production facilities in Georgia and Texas. Peanut products include commodities such as peanut butter and peanut paste, commonly used as ingredients in cookies, crackers, cereal, candy, ice cream, pet treats, and other foods. FDA reported that more than 3,900 products were recalled by more than 200 companies. During this outbreak, CDC identified 714 cases in 46 states, and according to CDC, the contamination may have contributed to the deaths of nine people. According to research from USDA's Economic Research Service, retail sales data indicate that, in the months following the initial CDC advisory on peanut products, demand declined for several months but returned to previous-year levels a few months later.

- A 2008 *outbreak of* Salmonella *Saintpaul associated with peppers from Mexico*, which sickened at least 1,440 people in 43 states and the District of Columbia and, according to a tomato industry representative, caused an estimated $145 million loss to tomato growers and shippers. Early in their work on this outbreak, government investigators identified a statistically significant association between consumption of certain types of tomatoes and illness. FDA's investigation subsequently confirmed the pathogen on samples of a pepper and in irrigation water from a farm in Mexico. A recall of tomatoes was never associated with this outbreak.

- A 2006 *outbreak of* E. coli *O157:H7 linked to fresh spinach from California.* FDA and the California Department of Public Health reported that this outbreak resulted in 205 confirmed illnesses and three deaths in 26 states. Industry representatives have reported that the outbreak caused an estimated $100 million loss to the spinach industry.

FDA is responsible for overseeing recalls of all food products under its jurisdiction. To carry out its responsibilities, FDA may issue advisories about adulterated food and may seek voluntary recalls by producers of food products; if a firm does not voluntarily recall a food product, FDA may use its new authority to order the recall of an article of food other than infant formula. Once a recall is under way, FDA monitors the effectiveness of a company's recall actions by verifying that customers in the food distribution chain receive notice of the recall and that the food is located and removed from the marketplace or that its labeling is corrected.[3] FDA can also take enforcement action, such as initiating the seizure of adulterated or misbranded products or levying civil monetary penalties against food companies under certain circumstances.

Many agencies, such as the following, play a role in responding to multistate outbreaks of foodborne illnesses:

- *Local and state governments*. Local agencies play two main roles: they (1) inspect food service and food retail establishments and (2) investigate cases of suspected foodborne illnesses, which may be reported to them by health care providers, clinical laboratories, or affected persons or someone close to them. State agencies also play a major part in identifying and investigating foodborne illnesses: state health departments typically receive and analyze routine disease surveillance reports, coordinate surveillance among local health departments, and report cases of foodborne illnesses to CDC.

- *CDC.* When CDC receives reports of outbreaks of foodborne illnesses from local and state governments, it determines the extent of an outbreak by linking cases or clusters of foodborne illnesses that have been reported. To make these links, it uses tools such as PulseNet[4] and the *Listeria* Initiative.[5] CDC then uses the medical science of epidemiology (which concerns the incidence, distribution, and control of disease and the factors affecting the presence or absence of a disease or pathogen) to identify the food associated with illnesses and

---

[3]We have reviewed FDA's oversight of food recalls twice since 2000. See GAO, *Food Safety: USDA and FDA Need to Better Ensure Prompt and Complete Recalls of Potentially Unsafe Food*, GAO-05-51 (Washington, D.C.: Oct. 6, 2004), and *Food Safety: Actions Needed by USDA and FDA to Ensure That Companies Promptly Carry Out Recalls*, GAO/RCED-00-195 (Washington, D.C.: Aug. 17, 2000).

[4]PulseNet is a network of state and local public health laboratories, as well as federal food regulatory laboratories, that performs molecular surveillance of foodborne infections by conducting DNA "fingerprinting" on bacteria and exchanging findings among laboratories. The network permits rapid comparison of these "fingerprint" patterns through an electronic database at CDC.

[5]The *Listeria* Initiative collects information on laboratory-confirmed cases of human listeriosis in the United States using a standardized, extended questionnaire to interview patients as cases are reported, rather than after clusters of cases are identified by public health professionals. According to CDC officials, this information, used in conjunction with data from PulseNet, allows professionals to more quickly identify epidemiologically related and nonrelated illnesses for further analysis.

provides that information to FDA. CDC also works with FDA to understand if the product's distribution can explain the observed geographic distribution of cases and to gather information on the root cause of the outbreak, to help prevent future problems.

- *FDA.* FDA participates in responding to outbreaks of foodborne illnesses by, among other things, participating in the epidemiologic investigation of the suspect food and conducting "traceback" investigations to determine how contamination occurred and, if applicable, which products should be recalled. The traceback process follows the product back through the supply chain to identify a common source.

In addition to us, other organizations have been tasked with reviewing FDA's oversight of food safety, including its public communications during foodborne illness outbreaks or recalls. Specifically, in 2007 Congress directed the Secretary of HHS to establish the Advisory Committee on Risk Communication (risk communication committee) to advise FDA on methods to effectively communicate risks associated with products regulated by the agency. In addition, the Institute of Medicine and the National Research Council, which are two of the four organizations in the National Academies,[6] published a report in 2010 on FDA's food safety oversight, including its public communications during events such as recalls or foodborne illness outbreaks.[7]

---

[6]The other two organizations are the National Academy of Sciences and National Academy of Engineering.

[7]Robert B. Wallace and Maria Oria, eds., *Enhancing Food Safety: The Role of the Food and Drug Administration* (Washington, D.C.: National Academies Press, 2010).

Several Key Entities Have Recall Authority, but FDA Has Not Issued Regulations or Industry Guidance on Its Ordering of Food Recalls

Several key federal, state, and international government entities, including FDA, have the authority to order product recalls. Under FSMA, FDA's process for ordering food recalls generally follows the same steps it and other federal agencies use to order recalls of other products. FDA has internal procedures describing the steps it will take to order a food recall, but these procedures are not yet public. Also, the agency has not issued regulations or industry guidance to clarify its ordered food recall process, and FDA officials told us that they have not decided whether they will do so and that FSMA contains no such requirement. In addition, FDA's ordered recall data for products other than food appear to be inconsistent or unreliable.

Entities with Authority to Order Product Recalls Use Processes with Similar Steps

Through our review, we identified several key government entities with the authority to order product recalls, including four federal agencies, at least four states, and at least five international government entities (see table 1). Officials from many of these entities reported, however, that ordered recalls are rare and that the majority of recalls are voluntary. Specifically, officials from the Consumer Product Safety Commission, the Environmental Protection Agency, and the National Highway Traffic Safety Administration reported no ordered recalls of products they oversee from fiscal year 2006 through fiscal year 2010. In addition, officials from several states and international entities we identified told us that they rarely use their authority to order product recalls. Officials from Texas told us that they use their authorities to order recalls in only the most extreme circumstances and officials from Canada said they use it as a last resort, such as when a company cannot be located to implement a voluntary recall. See table 1 for a list of the entities we identified as having the authority to order product recalls.

Table 1: Key Federal, State, and International Government Entities Having the Authority to Order Product Recalls

	Entity	Products
Federal agencies	Consumer Product Safety Commission	Many consumer goods
	Environmental Protection Agency	Vehicles and engines, pesticides
	FDA	Human biological products, foods within its jurisdiction (including infant formula[b]), medical devices, radiation-emitting electronic products, and tobacco products
	National Highway Traffic Safety Administration	Motor vehicles, child safety seats, tires, and other motor vehicle equipment
States[a]	Alaska	Foods
	New Mexico	
	South Carolina	
	Texas	
International entities[a]	Australia	Foods
	Canada	
	European Union	
	Japan	
	New Zealand	

Sources: GAO analysis of multiple sources (see app. I).

[a]The listed states and international entities represent those that we identified in our review as having authority to order a recall of food products or some specific type of food product (e.g., mi k or bottled water), and our list may not be comprehensive because we did not review statutes and regulations for all states and entities.

[b]FDA has had the authority to order infant formula recalls since 1986. If the Secretary of Health and Human Services determines that infant formula presents a risk to human health, the manufacturer must recall shipments immediately.

FDA's statutory process for ordering food recalls other than infant formula[8] includes three steps, which are also used by key federal agencies to order recalls of other product types. These steps are to

---

[8]In the wake of reports during 1979 that more than 100 infants became seriously ill as a consequence of using soybean-based formulas marketed with an insufficient amount of chloride, Congress passed the Infant Formula Act of 1980. This act established specific requirements for infant formulas—considered food under the Federal Food, Drug, and Cosmetic Act. The 1980 act established notification requirements and recall procedures when a manufacturer of an infant formula has reason to believe the infant formula fails to provide required nutrients or is otherwise adulterated or misbranded and presents a risk to human health. In 1986, these infant formula provisions were amended so that a recall of an infant formula would become mandatory if FDA determined the infant formula presented a risk to human health. Key differences between FDA's authority to order recalls of food and infant formula are noted in appendix II.

(1) determine that available evidence of a threat meets a specific standard of proof, (2) offer a company the opportunity to voluntarily recall a product before a recall order is issued, and (3) provide the company with an opportunity to challenge a recall decision. Specifically:

- *Standard of proof:* Before ordering a recall, each federal entity authorized to order product recalls is to determine—with a specified degree of certainty—that a problem exists. For example, before FDA may order a recall of food (other than infant formula), it is required by FSMA to determine that a reasonable probability exists that an article of food is adulterated under the Federal Food, Drug, and Cosmetic Act, or misbranded with respect to labeling for a major food allergen and that use of or exposure to that food will cause serious adverse health consequences or death to humans or animals. Similarly, the Environmental Protection Agency must first determine that certain vehicles or engines do not conform to emission standards before it may order a recall. In addition, to order a recall of motor vehicles or replacement equipment, the National Highway Traffic Safety Administration is to determine that a safety-related defect exists or that a product does not comply with an applicable motor vehicle safety standard.

- *Opportunity for voluntary recall.* For most products they oversee, the federal agencies we reviewed offer companies the chance to voluntarily recall product(s) in question before the agencies may order a recall. For example, for foods (other than infant formula), FDA is to provide companies an opportunity to cease distribution of the implicated food and recall it. Similarly, for medical devices, FDA is to provide companies an opportunity to consult with the agency, and companies can voluntarily recall the product before FDA may order a recall. In addition, after notifying a company of its determination that a product contains a defect which creates substantial risk of injury to the public, the Consumer Product Safety Commission provides the company an opportunity to voluntarily recall the product.

- *Opportunity to challenge the agency.* For most products they oversee, the federal agencies we reviewed are to provide an opportunity for companies to challenge an agency's decision to order a recall. For example, for foods (except infant formula), medical devices, and tobacco products, FDA is, by statute, to provide a company with an opportunity for an informal hearing on why the product in question should not be recalled. For licensed biological products, such as vaccines, the statute specifies that recall orders are subject to an agency hearing. However, there is no such requirement for infant formula recalls: FDA may determine that an infant formula presents a risk to human health, which would require that the company immediately take all actions necessary to recall the infant formula with no option for a hearing. At the National Highway Traffic Safety Administration, the agency is required to offer the company an opportunity to present information, views, and arguments that there is no defect or noncompliance before ordering a recall.

Figure 1 illustrates the steps required by statute for FDA's process of ordering food recalls (other than infant formula). For detailed descriptions of the ordered recall process for each federal agency we reviewed, see appendix II.

Figure 1: FDA's Statutorily Required Process for Ordering Food Recalls Other Than Infant Formula

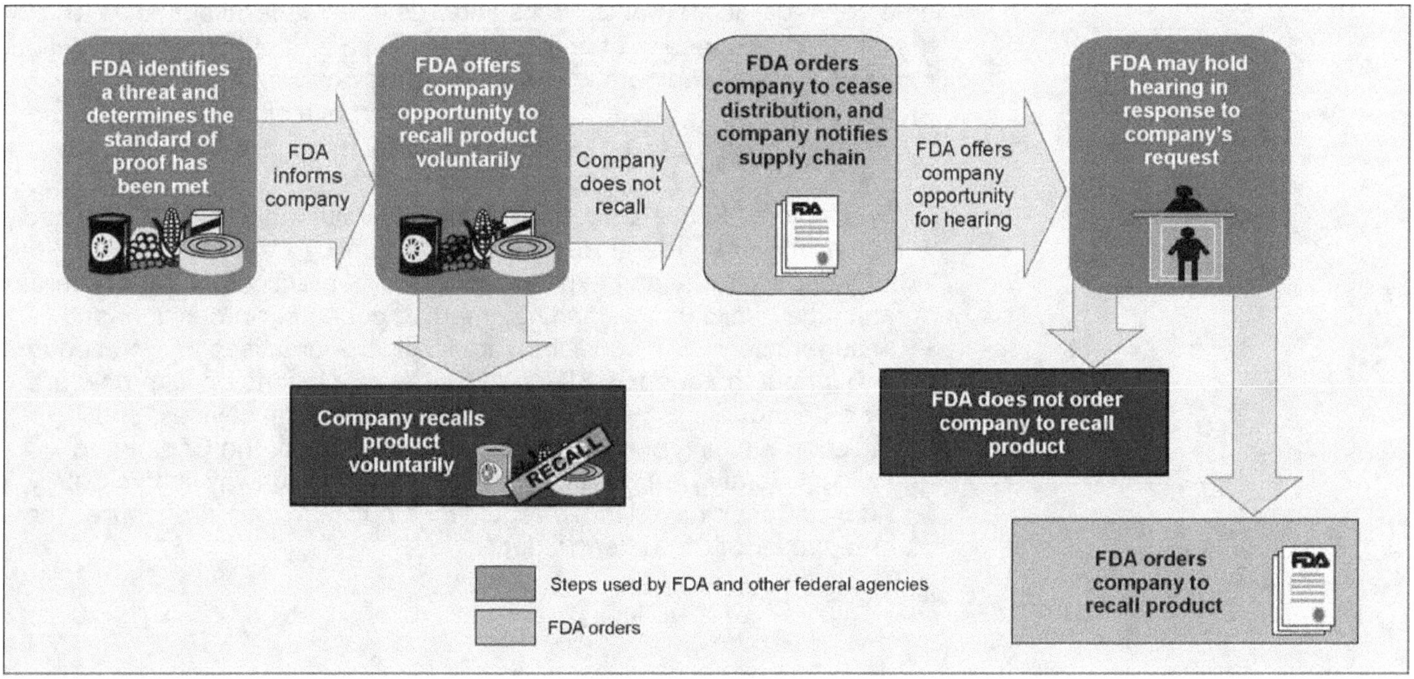

Source: GAO analysis of FDA Food Safety Modernization Act.

FDA Has Not Made Public Procedures for Ordering Food Recalls

FDA has interim internal procedures describing the steps it will take to order a food recall, but these procedures have not been made public, and the agency has not provided information on when they will be. Federal internal control standards call for federal agencies to clearly document policies, procedures, techniques, and mechanisms for implementing management directives and to make that documentation readily available for examination.[9] About a week-and-a-half before our closing meeting, FDA officials provided us interim internal procedures for ordering recalls of food. These interim procedures include detailed information on such topics as which officials are to be involved in an ordered food recall decision and what methods and timelines FDA officials will use to communicate with companies involved in such a recall. The interim procedures also state that FDA is to incorporate procedures into the agency's publicly available *Regulatory Procedures Manual* and other FDA documents. FDA officials have not, however, provided timelines on when they expect to make procedures publicly available.

Similarly, FDA officials told us that they have not decided whether they will issue regulations or industry guidance to clarify for the public FDA's procedures for ordering food recalls and that FSMA has no requirement to do so. Federal internal control standards direct federal agencies to ensure adequate means of communicating with and obtaining information from external stakeholders who may have a significant impact on the agency achieving its goals.[10] FDA and others have highlighted the value of clarifying procedures in regulations or industry guidance, as follows:

- *Regulations.* FDA's policy that applies to voluntary recalls is included in the Code of Federal Regulations. The policy states that it is intended to clarify and explain the agency's practices and procedures, enhance public understanding, improve consumer protection, and ensure uniform and consistent application of practices and procedures throughout the agency. FDA has issued regulations on its procedures for ordering recalls of biological products, medical devices, and radiation-emitting electronic products. In addition, the Consumer Product Safety Commission and the National Highway Traffic Safety Administration have issued regulations outlining their procedures for ordering recalls of other products.

---

[9]See GAO, *Standards for Internal Control in the Federal Government*, GAO/AIMD-00-21.3.1 (Washington, D.C.: November 1999). These standards, issued pursuant to the requirements of the Federal Managers' Financial Integrity Act of 1982, provide the overall framework for establishing and maintaining internal control in the federal government.

[10]GAO/AIMD-00-21.3.1.

- *Industry guidance.* FDA's good guidance practices[11] state that when significant changes are made to statute, the agency will review and, if appropriate, revise its guidance documents. These practices note that such changes reflect FDA's expectations of those subject to its oversight, including new expectations that may not be readily apparent—arguably the case with FDA's new authority to order food recalls: food industry stakeholders publicly asked FDA in June 2011 to explain how it will implement its new authority, indicating that they would benefit from more clarity. FDA's good guidance practices also indicate that guidance documents are subject to public comment and can be revised when appropriate. Nevertheless, FDA's current guidance for industry on voluntary product recalls has not been updated to describe the agency's procedures for ordering food recalls.

Furthermore, unlike other agencies with the authority to order product recalls, FDA has not documented—in internal agency procedures or its regulations or guidance—how it weighs evidence to determine if a food recall is warranted and thereby if it has met the standard of proof necessary to order a food recall. The following examples describe how other agencies with the authority to order product recalls have documented their investigation procedures, including how they weigh evidence on possible safety problems:

- The Consumer Product Safety Commission and National Highway Traffic Safety Administration have developed guidance to help stakeholders such as consumers and industry members understand how the agencies investigate and uncover problems that may lead to product recalls. These guidance documents also detail the types of evidence the agencies consider when determining whether a product poses safety risks or violates standards. For example, when reviewing whether a safety-related defect exists in a motor vehicle or related equipment, the National Highway Traffic Safety Administration's guidance notes that the agency will consider data on complaints, crashes, injuries, warranty claims, modifications, and part sales when conducting an investigation.

- Canadian public health and food safety agencies in 2011 published guidance on collecting and weighing evidence during outbreaks of

---

[11]Administrative Practices and Procedures: Good Guidance Practices, 65 Fed. Reg. 56,468 (Sept. 19, 2000) (codified at 21 C.F.R. § 10.115(k)(2)).

GAO-12-589 FDA's Food Advisory and Recall Process

foodborne illnesses to assist in deciding, among other things, whether a recall may be warranted.[12] Canadian officials published this guidance to provide criteria for, among other things, proceeding with a food recall. Officials told us that documenting procedures for weighing evidence can be helpful in answering questions from stakeholders about why they made a particular recall decision.

FDA has not gone as far as other agencies in explaining how the agency will weigh evidence to determine that a standard of proof has been met before ordering food recalls. FDA regulations state that the agency will conduct a health hazard evaluation for any product being considered for recall. In addition, FDA's interim procedures on ordered recalls do provide some information—including, for example, that officials from several FDA offices are to meet to determine whether the standard of proof for ordering a recall has been met. However, these regulations and procedures do not explain how FDA will weigh evidence to make that determination. We acknowledge, as an FDA official has pointed out, that each potential recall situation is different and requires that officials work with incomplete data to make decisions using the collective experience of seasoned professionals. Nevertheless, as the guidance from Canadian food safety agencies points out, documented procedures are intended to facilitate timely and appropriate actions by the agency, not to impose constraints. We also acknowledge that FDA has had the authority to order food recalls for a fairly short time—since FSMA was signed into law in January 2011. But without publicly available procedures, regulations, or industry guidance on how the agency will implement its authority—including how the agency will weigh evidence on whether a recall is necessary—the agency cannot ensure that it applies practices uniformly or consistently or that it provides clear information for the food industry to follow or consumers and the public to understand. Such ambiguity could be particularly troublesome with regard to outbreaks of foodborne illnesses, which can occur any time—indeed, have already occurred since FDA assumed its new authority—and demand clear and timely agency reactions.

---

[12]Health Canada, Public Health Agency of Canada, and Canadian Food Inspection Agency, *Weight of Evidence: Factors to Consider for Appropriate and Timely Action in a Foodborne Illness Outbreak Investigation* (Ottawa: January 2011).

FDA's Data on Ordered Recalls Appear to Be Unreliable

Since FSMA was signed into law in January 2011, FDA has not ordered any recalls of food products, according to agency officials. To learn more about ordered recalls for other products the agency oversees, we asked FDA officials for data on the number of ordered recalls of medical devices, radiation-emitting electronic products, and biological products, and we received conflicting information. Specifically, when we asked officials for the total number of ordered recalls in the agency's history, FDA officials from different offices within the agency provided us with inconsistent data that appeared to be insufficiently reliable for public reporting. Examples include the following:

- *Biological products.* Officials from FDA's Center for Biologics Evaluation and Research—the center that regulates biological products for human use—told us there were two ordered recalls in 2006 and one in the 1980s. Officials from FDA's Office of Regulatory Affairs—the office that manages the agency's central recall database known as the Recall Enterprise System—told us there were two ordered recalls of biological products in the agency's history according to this database. Later, however, officials from the Office of Regulatory Affairs and the Center for Biologics Evaluation and Research stated that their counts were in error, explaining that the two events in fiscal year 2006 were not ordered recalls but, rather, orders for companies to cease manufacturing. These officials later provided us with information on a single ordered recall that took place in fiscal year 2002.

- *Medical devices and radiation-emitting electronic products.* Officials from FDA's Office of Regulatory Affairs told us there were nine ordered recalls in the agency's history, with no such recalls occurring from fiscal years 2006 through 2010 according to data in the Recall Enterprise System. Officials from FDA's Center for Devices and Radiological Health also told us there were nine ordered recalls in the agency's history, but three of these occurred from fiscal years 2006 through 2010.

We asked FDA officials to clarify these issues and received some responses, but the information they provided did not clarify all observed inconsistencies in the data. (For more information on the inconsistencies and inaccuracies we identified, see app. III.)

According to FDA's *Regulatory Procedures Manual*, its Recall Enterprise System allows the agency to (1) provide a central, searchable database to efficiently track information and generate and disseminate reports of recall activities; (2) increase communication of recall information among different FDA offices; and (3) reduce duplication of efforts across different FDA offices, among other things. In addition, under federal internal control standards,[13] federal agencies are to employ controls over information processing; such control includes application control, which is designed to help ensure completeness and accuracy of a system's data, among other things. Nevertheless, the inconsistencies we observed in the data caused us to question the Recall Enterprise System's data on ordered recalls. Moreover, our review also showed that FDA used multiple data systems, which may lead to inconsistencies in its data if controls over information processing are not in place. Both of these issues limit the agency's ability to use the Recall Enterprise System to meet the database's goals to efficiently track information, communicate recall information among different FDA offices, and reduce duplication of effort across offices. These issues also indicate that the agency may not have sufficient internal control for its information processing, reducing the agency's ability to accurately report information on ordered recalls to Congress and the public as follows:

- *The Recall Enterprise System's categories for ordered recalls do not have documented definitions, leading to incomplete and inaccurate data.* When entering information on an ordered recall into the agency's data system, FDA staff can choose from several categories of ordered recalls. Our analysis indicated several problems with these categories. For example, the list of ordered recall categories is incomplete because the system currently does not include categories for ordered recalls of infant formula or tobacco products. In addition, a few categories are inaccurate: two of the categories—"FDA requested" and "FDA ordered seizure"—are not ordered recalls. When we reviewed the user guide and data dictionary[14] for the Recall Enterprise System, we were unable to find written definitions for categories of ordered recalls, without which FDA officials cannot be sure that users consistently apply the same information when categorizing a recall. When we talked to FDA officials about this issue, they acknowledged these problems and told us that they are leading a

---

[13]GAO/AIMD-00-21.3.1.

[14]A data dictionary is a centralized repository of information about data in a database such as its meaning, relationships to other data, origin, usage, and format.

team to evaluate the definitions of these categories and instructions for FDA staff on the use of each category.

- *The databases that contain recall data do not fully share information.* FDA officials told us they use multiple databases to track recall data and, because some of the databases do not fully share data, staff must sometimes enter data into the Recall Enterprise System and then reenter the same data into another database. The fact that these databases do not have a two-way connection to ensure that all inputs are received in the Recall Enterprise System could have led to some of the inconsistencies we noted and runs counter to FDA's goal of having its central system reduce duplication of effort among FDA offices. We have reported on similar issues in the past. In October 2004, we reported that FDA's Center for Food Safety and Applied Nutrition, which is responsible for protecting the public's health by ensuring that food within FDA's jurisdiction is safe, sanitary, wholesome, and honestly labeled, maintained its own database outside of the Recall Enterprise System.[15] We also reported that (1) inconsistencies between the Recall Enterprise System and the Center for Food Safety and Applied Nutrition's system raised significant questions about the validity and reliability of the data and that (2) FDA's investment of more than $3 million to implement the Recall Enterprise System would not be entirely realized until the agency used the system as the only one for collecting and managing recall data. As a result, we recommended that FDA direct the food recall staff to use the Recall Enterprise System as the sole data system to capture recall information, manage food recalls, and generate reports to Congress. In response, FDA officials told us that they would implement this recommendation, but in September 2008 we again reported that staff in the Center for Food Safety and Applied Nutrition continued to maintain a separate unofficial database for food recalls.[16] FDA once again agreed to use the Recall Enterprise System as its sole recall data system. In a February 2010 report, we identified modernizing information systems as a major management challenge

---

[15]GAO-05-51.

[16]GAO, *Food Labeling: FDA Needs to Better Leverage Resources, Improve Oversight, and Effectively Use Available Data to Help Consumers Select Healthy Foods,* GAO-08-597 (Washington, D.C.: Sept. 9, 2008).

that could affect FDA's ability to carry out its mission.[17] A survey we conducted for that report showed that 79 percent of FDA managers reported that improving FDA's information technology and information management would greatly improve their ability to contribute to FDA's goals and responsibilities, but 39 percent reported that FDA was making great progress in this area.[18] Furthermore, when we asked FDA managers in that survey to identify the top priorities that FDA leadership should address, improving information technology was the third most commonly identified issue.[19] In March 2012, we reported that the Center for Food Safety and Applied Nutrition maintains 21 different databases and systems and had not adequately assessed data-sharing opportunities.[20] We recommended that the agency assess the center's information sharing needs and capabilities to identify potential improvements to achieve more efficient information sharing among databases and develop a plan for implementing these improvements. During our present review, we asked officials in the Center for Food Safety and Applied Nutrition why they continue to maintain a database separate from the Recall Enterprise System, and the officials responded that in certain cases, the center's database was easier to search than the Recall Enterprise System.

---

[17]GAO, *Food and Drug Administration: Opportunities Exist to Better Address Management Challenges*, GAO-10-279 (Washington, D.C.: Feb. 19, 2010).

[18]GAO, *Food and Drug Administration: 2009 FDA Managers Survey on Performance and Management Issues, an E-supplement to* GAO-10-279, GAO-10-280SP (Washington, D.C.: Feb. 19, 2010).

[19]The first most commonly identified issue was, "recruiting, retaining, and developing a workforce with the knowledge, skills, and abilities necessary to carry out its mission." The second most commonly identified issue was, "improving coordination and communication within FDA."

[20]GAO, *Information Technology: FDA Needs to Fully Implement Key Management Practices to Lessen Modernization Risks*, GAO-12-346 (Washington D.C.: Mar. 15, 2012).

GAO-12-589 FDA's Food Advisory and Recall Process

FDA Has Taken Steps to Begin Meeting Communication Challenges When Advising the Public about Food Recalls and Outbreaks

FDA faces a number of communication challenges when it needs to advise the public about food recalls and outbreaks of foodborne illness, ranging from balancing technical accuracy with timeliness of communications to coordinating messages with other agencies to meeting the needs of diverse public audiences, such as consumers, representatives of the food industry, medical professionals, and other government organizations. The agency has taken several steps to begin meeting these challenges but has yet to fully adopt recommendations from us and others to develop a comprehensive food recall communication policy and related implementation plans.

FDA Faces Challenges in Seven Related Categories and Has Taken Some Steps to Address Them

Through publications from FDA and the National Academies, meeting materials of FDA's risk communication committee, and our own past work, as well as interviews with government officials, experts, and stakeholders, our review identified seven communications challenges FDA faces in advising the public about food recalls and outbreaks. These challenges include (1) balancing the goals of timeliness and accuracy, (2) using precise language while being understandable to a general audience, (3) serving a wide range of audiences and audience needs, (4) maintaining public trust in FDA communications, (5) coordinating messages with other agencies, (6) testing draft communications with users, and (7) communicating when an outbreak or recall is over. To address these challenges, FDA has taken numerous actions, as outlined in the agency's *Strategic Plan for Risk Communication*[21] and other sources.

Balancing the Goals of Timeliness and Accuracy

During an outbreak or recall, FDA faces the challenge of quickly providing information to the public about the event, often as the event is unfolding and information about its cause is evolving, while also being accurate and specific. FDA officials, as well as the experts and stakeholders we spoke with, widely agreed that this challenge was the most important one confronting FDA when advising the public about food recalls and outbreaks. To make determinations about what information to provide and when to provide it, FDA officials told us that they use professional experience to look for a "tipping point," that is, a time when evidence collected from a variety of sources—including epidemiological studies (which form and test hypotheses about an outbreak's cause), field

---

[21]Department of Health and Human Services, Food and Drug Administration, *Strategic Plan for Risk Communication* (Silver Spring, MD: Fall 2009).

investigations, and laboratory results—is sufficient to allow the agency to provide consumers with information that will help them avoid unsafe food. FDA officials also stated that it is often only in hindsight, when all information is known, that they can confidently say when the right time was to provide what type of information. For example, officials said, they are sometimes criticized for providing information after other entities, such as state agencies, have already done so. The officials explained that FDA must use well-developed evidence when deciding whether to advise the public about a food safety issue. Conversely, during a 2006 outbreak of *E. coli* associated with fresh bagged spinach, FDA officials advised consumers to avoid eating fresh spinach before they knew specifically which brands were implicated. FDA officials said they took this action to protect consumers, but spinach industry representatives reported suffering economic harm from FDA's advisory.

FDA has taken steps to address this challenge. For example, in September 2011, the agency announced the formation of the Coordinated Outbreak Response and Evaluation (CORE) network, staffed with several full-time FDA employees focused on preparing for, coordinating, and carrying out responses to foodborne illness outbreaks. Before establishing the CORE network, FDA officials said, the agency responded to outbreak events by bringing staff together on an ad hoc basis; according to FDA documentation, the CORE network aims to improve the agency's response to outbreaks, as well as the speed and accuracy of its public communications. In addition, FDA officials told us that they are creating an expedited clearance process for outbreak-related advisories and that they hope this process will allow FDA to prepare and issue advisories within 6 hours, rather than the current time frame that ranges from 24 hours to 3 days. As of April 20, 2012, FDA had not finalized this process.

Providing Precise, Complete Information Understandable to a General Audience

FDA faces the following two related challenges in this area:

- *Technical precision.* According to FDA officials, the precision sought by scientists and attorneys for the agency's public communications can result in highly technical language that may not be understandable to a general audience. To address this issue, FDA has used input from its risk communication committee to create a template for its recall press releases. According to FDA, the template helps to provide more consumer-friendly information and includes for each recall specifics on the problem, symptoms of illness, and what consumers or others can do to protect themselves. In addition, FDA's *Strategic Plan for Risk Communication* states that the agency plans to regularly review documents provided to the public to ensure that they use plain language and are geared to target audiences' reading levels; the agency requires each operating unit to report annually on its implementation of this effort. When we requested information on these annual implementation reports, however, we learned that FDA had not produced any.

- *Large amounts of information.* FDA must sometimes provide large amounts of information on the types and number of products involved in a recall or outbreak. For example, during the 2010 outbreak of *Salmonella* associated with shell eggs, the implicated eggs came from two producers. These producers, however, sold their eggs to other companies, which then marketed the eggs under at least 46 separate brand names or used the eggs as ingredients in other foods. Similarly, according to FDA's website, a 2008-2009 outbreak of *Salmonella* associated with peanut products led to a recall of more than 3,900 products because the peanut products in question had been used as ingredients in many foods. To address this challenge, FDA has provided searchable databases on its website of products affected by such recalls for several prior outbreaks, including the 2010 outbreak of *Salmonella* associated with shell eggs and the 2008-2009 outbreak of *Salmonella* associated with peanut products.[22]

Serving a Wide Range of Audiences and Audience Needs

FDA officials reported that the agency serves a variety of audiences—including consumers; industry organizations such as producers, distributors, and retailers; medical professionals; and other governmental organizations, such as states—all with different needs and uses for food safety information. FDA has taken actions to address this challenge. For example, in accordance with FSMA requirements, FDA redesigned its recalls website in April 2011, which, according to FDA, now contains a more consumer-friendly search engine, with search results displayed in a table of food recalls since 2009 by date, product brand name, product description, reason for recall, and recalling company. FDA also posts photos of recalled products affected by Class I and high-priority Class II

---

[22]See http://www.accessdata.fda.gov/scripts/shelleggsrecall/ for the 2010 shell egg recall products database and http://www.accessdata.fda.gov/scripts/peanutbutterrecall/index.cfm for the 2008-2009 peanut products recall database.

recalls on its website.[23] In addition, according to an FDA website, the agency has committed to support industry efforts to enable consumers to distinguish recalled products from those not subject to a recall. For example, during a recall of pistachio products in 2009, FDA's website provided a link to an industry-sponsored website listing companies whose products did not contain recalled pistachios. Third, FDA officials reported increased use of blogs and other social media to communicate with the public and, according to these officials, offer information in multiple languages.

Maintaining Public Trust in FDA Communications

FDA officials reported that if the public does not see the agency as trusted and credible, its communications will be less effective. FDA is undertaking efforts to address this challenge. For example, according to FDA's *Strategic Plan for Risk Communication*, the agency plans to (1) regularly monitor the Internet for non-FDA websites that misleadingly report FDA information and (2) develop talking points, where appropriate, to address such misleading communications. In addition, FDA officials told us that the agency intends for the leader of its CORE network to serve as the main agency spokesperson during outbreaks. According to our review of risk communication committee meeting transcripts, a few members of this committee agree that having a single spokesperson creates a recognizable face for the agency, which could improve public trust and understanding.

Coordinating Messages with Other Agencies

According to experts and stakeholders from state and local health and agriculture departments, not having systematic communication, including communication between governmental agencies and the public, is a key challenge in creating an effective food safety system. They noted that, in some cases, when many agencies are involved in responding to an outbreak of foodborne illness, these agencies may deliver to the public as many messages as there are agencies, which can cause confusion. In addition, a 2010 National Academies study by the Institute of Medicine

---

[23]As part of their recall programs, both FDA and USDA classify recalls on the basis of their severity. Class I recalls present the greatest risk to human health: they cover situations where there is a reasonable probability that the use or exposure to the product will cause serious adverse health consequences or death and may involve food contaminated with disease-causing bacteria, such as *Listeria* or *Salmonella*, or foods containing a major food allergen such as nuts or eggs, not identified on the label. Class II and Class III recalls involve foods from which the risk of adverse health consequences is remote or not likely, respectively. For example, according to FDA documentation, a Class III recall might include a lack of English labeling on a food product.

and National Research Council reported that consumers are unaware of the frequency of food recalls and have misconceptions about the division of responsibilities between federal agencies. This challenge is not unique to FDA's communications during food-related outbreaks or recalls. In a February 2010 report, we identified coordinating internally and externally as a major management challenge that could affect FDA's ability to carry out its mission.[24] In a survey we conducted for that report, we showed that 49 percent of FDA managers reported that improved coordination and communication with other governmental entities would improve their ability to contribute to meeting FDA's goals and responsibilities, and 19 percent reported great progress in improving coordination and communication with other federal agencies.[25]

To address cross-agency coordination, FDA has undertaken several efforts. For example, in 2011, FDA signed a memorandum of understanding with USDA to provide a framework for the two agencies to communicate and cooperate in the timely and full exchange of information, and FDA officials told us that they meet weekly with officials from both USDA and CDC to discuss outbreaks and recalls reported by FoodSafety.gov—a website that disseminates food safety information and alerts consumers about food outbreaks and recalls. In addition, FDA officials told us that they formally share press releases with CDC, and that FDA informally shares press releases with USDA and the Environmental Protection Agency. Such frequent communications among collaborating agencies are consistent with what we reported in October 2005 that can facilitate working across agency boundaries and prevent misunderstandings.[26] With respect to better coordination with states, in 2011, FDA and a group of state-level officials developed a draft guide on improving federal-state communications during outbreaks.

Testing Draft Communications with Users

According to an FDA publication, effective communication requires understanding and addressing audience needs that can be identified only by talking with targeted audiences. Members of FDA's risk communication committee stated that testing is very important because it is difficult to know how a communication will be understood by those

---

[24]GAO-10-279.

[25]GAO-10-280SP.

[26]GAO, *Results-Oriented Government: Practices That Can Help Enhance and Sustain Collaboration among Federal Agencies*, GAO-06-15 (Washington, D.C.: Oct. 15, 2005).

receiving it unless it is tested. For example, during the 2011 outbreak of *Listeria* associated with cantaloupes, a watermelon industry representative stated that FDA officials used the generic term "melon," rather than "cantaloupe," in some of its early communications on the outbreak, and this term might have been interpreted to include all melons, creating losses for the watermelon industry. Testing before releasing communications might uncover this type of issue. To do such testing however, FDA must comply with the Paperwork Reduction Act, which requires that it submit to a formal clearance process through the Office of Management and Budget (OMB) before it can obtain information from 10 or more individuals. To address this challenge, FDA has taken a few actions. First, in 2010, the agency established an internal network of FDA employees to review draft messages before they are released publicly. Second, in 2010, FDA officials said that they requested OMB approval for a "generic" clearance that would allow the agency to test (using focus groups) food-safety-related messages, and in June 2012, the agency announced that it had received approval from OMB on that clearance.

Communicating When an Outbreak or Recall Is Over

FDA's *Strategic Plan for Risk Communication* reported that once a recall is over, effective communication is needed to assure consumers that it is once again safe to consume a previously recalled or implicated product. The plan also stated that consumers do not always know that a recall or outbreak has ended and may continue to avoid affected foods. An FDA official stated that it can be difficult for the agency to know when implicated products are no longer a danger and a recall may be over, since some products may mistakenly remain for sale for a very long time or sit on consumers' shelves. To address this issue, an FDA report, as well as a report by the Institute of Medicine and National Research Council—both produced in June 2010—recommended the agency reconsider its policy, stating that if FDA determines that a recall is terminated, this information should be disclosed to the public. FDA officials told us that they are reviewing options for addressing this challenge but that they have not made any changes to their policies.

FDA Has Not Fully Adopted Some Recommended Communication Policies or Plans Related to Identified Challenges

Beyond the steps it has taken to date, FDA has not implemented several recommendations that could help the agency better respond to its communication challenges. Specifically, it has not (1) adopted a 2009 recommendation from its risk communication committee on creating a policy for emerging events to more comprehensively address all its communication challenges; (2) created plans recommended in 2010 by the Institute of Medicine and National Research Council to help address coordination challenges surrounding its communications; or (3) fully implemented a recommendation from our past work to determine jointly with USDA what, if any, additional approaches are needed for alerting consumers about recalls. When we asked FDA officials how they had responded to these recommendations, they provided us information on some actions they are taking. However, FDA's stated actions do not fully implement these recommendations. As a result of FDA's not taking full action on these recommendations, the agency may be missing opportunities to more comprehensively address the challenges it faces.

FDA has not implemented a 2009 recommendation from its risk communication committee to create a communication policy for use during emerging events, including outbreaks of foodborne illness and large-scale food recalls. The committee recommended that such a policy and resulting communications address several topics, including the nature of potential risks and benefits of a product, the quality of the agency's evidence, actions that might be taken by vulnerable populations, and actions that FDA is taking. The committee stated that, over time, such a policy would help make FDA's actions increasingly predictable and its communications better understood. Ideally, according to the committee, by developing useful and timely communications and monitoring the effects of those communications, FDA would enable individuals to follow emerging events, take protective action, or decide that no action was needed. During our review, we contacted a former member of the committee, who told us that implementing this recommendation could help the agency make progress with respect to several of the communication challenges we identified, including, for example, balancing the goals of timeliness and accuracy and maintaining public trust in FDA communications. When we asked FDA officials about whether they had implemented this recommendation, they told us that the agency is working toward creating communications that are as consistent as possible, subject to differences between the types of products the agency oversees. In addition, FDA has created a checklist for FDA staff to use when developing public communications. According to FDA, this checklist is intended to help specify roles and responsibilities of different FDA experts in communications development. Nevertheless, the checklist does not include information on the topics recommended by the risk communication committee. It also does not clarify for those outside the agency what to expect from FDA communications.

In addition to not implementing the risk communication committee's recommendation, FDA has not developed plans to address its coordination challenges when providing public information, as previously recommended by the Institute of Medicine and National Research

Council. In response to a congressional request, the institute and council in 2010 published a report on FDA's food safety oversight in which the institute and council recommended that FDA create, in conjunction with other federal agencies, a coordinated plan for communicating with affected parties during crises. According to FDA officials, the agency expressed appreciation for the efforts of those involved in producing the report and would consider the report's recommendations. However, the agency has not developed a concrete plan to improve such coordination; thus the agency continues to risk providing information on foodborne illnesses that conflicts with the information provided by other agencies or confuses consumers who may receive conflicting messages from several sources.

Furthermore, FDA has not fully implemented a recommendation from our October 2004 report,[27] in which we reviewed recall communications at both FDA and USDA and stated that the procedures both agencies use to advise consumers of a recall—press releases and web postings—may not be effective. We recommended that FDA work jointly with USDA to determine what, if any, additional approaches were needed for advising consumers about recalls. To show us how they had responded to this recommendation, FDA officials provided us a copy of recall response guidelines issued by the Coalition to Improve Foodborne Outbreak Response—a working group of federal agencies including FDA, USDA, and CDC, along with associations of state and local health professionals. These guidelines provide broad advice to agencies on improving communication with the public during a recall, but they do not address the two public notification topics we discussed in detail in our 2004 report—posting recall press releases on agency websites and providing information on the retail outlets that received recalled food. We followed up with USDA and FDA on these two topics and learned that USDA's public notifications have changed but that FDA's have not, as follows:

- *Posting recall information on agency websites.* Both FDA and USDA post recall press releases on their websites. According to USDA guidelines, USDA authors its own releases, while our review of FDA web postings indicated that the agency often posts releases that are crafted by the companies issuing the recall rather than issuing its own information on the recall. A representative of a consumer organization

---

[27]GAO-05-51.

testified before FDA's risk communication committee that FDA does not have full control of the message sent to the public when it does not issue its own press releases. For example, industry press releases often note that they are "voluntarily" recalling a product. Such statements may be technically correct, but a representative of a consumer organization testified before FDA's risk communication committee that such statements may cause consumers to underestimate the seriousness of a recall. In addition, FDA's own Transparency Initiative—an FDA effort to identify and implement actions to increase transparency—reported in May 2010 that FDA is in the best position to ensure that useful, actionable information is provided to the public about a problem with an FDA-regulated product. During a meeting of FDA's risk communication committee in November 2010, several committee members stated that FDA's practice of posting and relying on industry releases for recall information could decrease public trust in FDA communications.

- *Providing information on the retail outlets that received recalled food.* As we reported in 2004, FDA and USDA stated that the agencies generally do not have the authority to provide information on the retail stores selling a recalled food because it is considered confidential business information. In 2008, however, USDA changed its policy: the department now collects and posts public information on which retail outlets received products associated with recalls posing the most serious health risks.[28] Further, in its technical comments to our draft report, HHS stated that FDA can provide confidential commercial information, including the identity of a retail store associated with products implicated in a recall, if such information is necessary to effect a recall.

By not fully addressing our recommendation, specifically concerning the two public notification topics we discussed in detail in our 2004 report, FDA has missed opportunities to work with USDA to learn from its experiences with public communications during recalls. We continue to believe that FDA is missing opportunities to strengthen the effectiveness of its procedures to advise consumers of a recall and that FDA can learn from USDA's experiences with public communications during recalls.

---

[28]USDA posts information on its website as to which retail outlets receive products associated with Class I recalls.

GAO-12-589 FDA's Food Advisory and Recall Process

Several Mechanisms Might be Available to Compensate the Food Industry for Erroneously Ordered Recalls or Erroneous Food-Related Advisories

Individuals we interviewed identified a variety of government mechanisms—each with advantages and disadvantages described by the individuals—that might be available to compensate food producers in case of an erroneously ordered food recall or erroneous food-related advisory, but we found no examples of such mechanisms being used to provide compensation. Among others, these mechanisms include a dedicated government program and government insurance. Individuals we interviewed also identified several factors that may come into play when deciding to establish any new compensation mechanism, such as defining what constitutes an error or mitigating the potential for unintended consequences.

Each Compensation Mechanism Has Advantages and Disadvantages

Through a series of interviews with stakeholders and others, including representatives of consumer groups and industry organizations, federal and state officials, and experts in food safety or food law, as well as our review of relevant literature, we identified a variety of government mechanisms that others have suggested might compensate the food industry in case of an erroneously ordered food recall or erroneous food-related advisory, each with advantages and disadvantages described by those we interviewed. We did not independently evaluate the viability of these mechanisms, their advantages, or their disadvantages, and none of the mechanisms has been used to provide compensation in such instances. The first of the mechanisms described below has an established government structure in place to administer it; the others would require congressional action to initiate.

The Judicial Process

Individuals have suggested that remedies may be available through the judicial process, a mechanism that already exists. At least one company—a South Carolina tomato farm—filed suit against the federal government for FDA's 2008 warning of an apparent link between eating raw red tomatoes and a *Salmonella* outbreak. The government responded by asserting, among other things, that FDA is immune to the particular claim. A few respondents have told us that the judicial process might allow for cases to be handled individually, which would allow each plaintiff a chance to be heard and for each case to be decided on its merits. Assuming a filed claim is valid, however, some others told us that the judicial process can be slow and expensive. In the case of erroneously ordered recalls or advisories, for example, smaller companies could be heavily burdened with the costs of bringing suit against the federal government.

A Dedicated Program

A federal program established by Congress could pay eligible companies, according to the relevant literature and our interviews with stakeholders and others. For example, at USDA, the Animal and Plant Health Inspection Service (APHIS) administers a series of programs that compensate producers whom APHIS orders to destroy their cattle to control or eradicate disease. The APHIS program implements cost sharing with the states and may pay producers from 50 to 100 percent of the animals' market value in compensation. An APHIS official told us that the reason for such compensation is to encourage producers to participate in the programs. Some respondents also identified government purchase programs of food commodities, such as USDA's National School Lunch Program, as a possible dedicated program that could offer producers another avenue for selling their food. USDA purchases food products through commodity purchase programs in support of the National School Lunch Program and the School Breakfast Program. One respondent suggested it may be possible to amend the current programs to assign preference to particular growers who were affected by an erroneously ordered recall or advisory, as long as the products were determined to be safe.

Some respondents said that a potential advantage of a dedicated program would be the assurance to industry that a formal mechanism would be available to compensate them in the event of an erroneously ordered recall or advisory. Further, according to a few respondents, a dedicated program could allow eligibility requirements to be set up ahead of time, providing a structured method for determining compensation. In addition, according to a few respondents, an advantage of this mechanism would be that it could be administered by an agency other than FDA, which could help FDA avoid spending resources administering a compensation program (a source of concern for stakeholders from consumer organizations). On the other hand, respondents also noted disadvantages. For example, some told us that in lean budget times, funding for such a program may be difficult to obtain. A few others stated that setting up a system to administer the program could take significant time and resources. Specific to the suggestion to modify current government purchase programs, one respondent observed that selling erroneously recalled produce to schools may not be a popular policy with school boards or parents.

One-Time Funding for Specific Events

Congress could consider a one-time legislative act for specific events as a mechanism to provide one-time funding for affected industry members after a specific instance of an erroneous food recall or advisory, according to the relevant literature and our interviews with stakeholders and others.

For example, Congress considered a bill in 2008 that proposed $100 million in emergency assistance to tomato growers and handlers to address losses associated with FDA's 2008 advisory related to the *Salmonella* outbreak first linked to tomatoes then later to peppers. In another example, member states of the European Commission (one of the main institutions of the European Union that manages the day-to-day business of implementing European Union policies and spending its funds) agreed to provide €227 million in emergency funding to support the vegetable producers who suffered losses due to an *E. coli* outbreak in spring 2011, according to commission press documents. In this instance, German health officials had originally identified cucumbers, raw tomatoes, and lettuce as significantly associated with the outbreak but later linked the outbreak to bean sprouts. In this case, a European Union official told us that the European Commission provided aid to farmers who were suffering financially and that this aid was not intended as compensation for government error.

Several respondents told us that an advantage of one-time funding for specific events would be that compensation could be tailored to each erroneously ordered recall or erroneous food-related advisory. But several stakeholders also said that a disadvantage of a one-time legislative act for specific events is that such an act is inherently subject to political realities. For example, companies growing specialty crops in only one location in the country could have more trouble garnering broad-based political support than a group of larger growers who produce crops in many parts of the country. Further, some respondents said that it could take a long time for such funding to work its way through the legislative process, which could create difficulties for food producers, and that such a program could be expensive for government to administer.

Government Insurance

If established by Congress, government insurance could help mitigate companies' losses, according to the relevant literature and our interviews with stakeholders and others. For example, USDA subsidizes federal crop insurance premiums, helping food producers mitigate the risk of losing (1) revenue because of either market fluctuations or extreme weather and (2) crops because of extreme weather.[29] In this program, backed by the

---

[29]For more information on crop insurance, see GAO, *Crop Insurance: Savings Would Result from Program Changes and Greater Use of Data Mining*, GAO-12-256 (Washington, D.C.: Mar. 13, 2012), and GAO, *Crop Insurance: Opportunities Exist to Reduce the Costs of Administering the Program*, GAO-09-445 (Washington, D.C.: Apr. 29, 2009).

federal government, producers pay premiums that are, in aggregate, lower than the amount needed to cover expected claims. As a result, the federal government is subsidizing the balance. According to USDA officials, the policies do not cover losses related to either an erroneously ordered recall or an erroneous food-related advisory. Federal crop insurance covers most major crops, such as corn and wheat, against these natural disasters, but insurance coverage for more specialized crops, such as fruits and vegetables, is generally available in the primary growing areas for those crops.[30] USDA offers coverage only if it can find there is sufficient actuarial data in each county to provide insurance. A few food safety experts have suggested that a specific type of crop insurance called Adjusted Gross Revenue (AGR) might cover losses associated with price drops or a reduction in demand due to a foodborne illness outbreak. However, USDA officials told us that, as with other forms of federal crop insurance, AGR does not cover losses related to an erroneously ordered recall or an erroneous food-related advisory. Further, crop insurance policies cover only producers, not suppliers, distributors, or other companies in the distribution chain.[31] In addition to a government insurance program, we identified private-sector options and learned that the private sector does offer policies to insure against losses from recalls; a few respondents, however, told us that these policies may be cost-prohibitive for some companies. Further, according to private-sector insurance representatives we contacted, private insurance policies typically do not cover losses to companies whose food products are not adulterated but that may instead suffer "collateral damage" from declines in prices for their products; such collateral damage could result if or when consumers stop purchasing any product for which the government ordered a recall or issued a food-related advisory. Similarly, as one respondent stated, no private-sector policies cover damages for

---

[30]On June 19, 2012, the United States Senate voted to amend the Senate's proposed 2012 Farm Bill to require that USDA submit a report to the House Committee on Agriculture and the Senate Committee on Agriculture, Nutrition, and Forestry evaluating insurance policies and plans that provide protection for production or revenue affected by food safety concerns, including those that result in advisories or recalls. This report would determine whether offering such policies for specialized crops, such as fruits and vegetables, would benefit agricultural producers. See 158 Cong. Rec. S4276 (daily ed. June 19, 2012) (vote on amendment 2309 amending Agriculture Reform, Food, and Jobs Act of 2012, S. 3240, 112th Cong, § 11017).

[31]In the Federal Crop Insurance Act, "producer" is defined as a "'person" (as defined by the Secretary of Agriculture) who is 18 years of age and has a bona fide insurable interest in a crop as an owner-operator, landlord, tenant, or sharecropper. 7 U.S.C. § 1520.

advisories (rather than recalls), perhaps, as insurance literature indicates, because a large number of claims could be filed at the same time, resulting in potentially catastrophic losses for insurers. In addition to traditional insurance, one respondent suggested that the use of a "check-off" program—in which a group of producers creates a form of self-insurance (not government subsidized)—could help producers mitigate the risk of broader market effects from a recall or advisory. Under such a program, companies could pay a set amount (e.g., per production unit) into a fund, which could then be used to pay participants if the market experienced a decline in consumer demand resulting from a recall or advisory.

A few respondents said that a potential advantage of government insurance programs is that they may be relatively easy to implement because the agricultural sector is familiar with them, and one respondent stated the infrastructure to administer such programs already exists. Further, according to a few respondents, government insurance provides clear criteria and guidance to develop a program in advance of when it might be needed. One disadvantage, however, is that, as with any insurance program, insured participants might take greater risks if they were no longer entirely responsible for losses due to those risks, a concept referred to as "moral hazard." Another challenge to managing insurance programs arises when people who face higher risks enroll in greater numbers than those who face lower risks, increasing the likelihood that the insurer will pay more in claims, a concept termed "adverse selection."

In addition, insurance premiums could be difficult to calculate because the expected behavior of those purchasing insurance and the risks of erroneous government actions are not well known.[32] For example, one respondent said it could be difficult for insurers to calculate actuarially sound premiums for insurance in the case of erroneously ordered recalls or erroneous food-related advisories. One reason is that if a policyholder adopts risky agricultural practices, he or she may increase the likelihood that the insurer will have to pay a claim, which creates difficulties in assessing the likelihood that a policy will have to pay. Further, economists

---

[32]For more on the difficulty of charging premiums that fully reflect risks, see our reports on the National Flood Insurance Program, such as GAO, *Flood Insurance: Public Policy Goals Provide a Framework for Reform*, GAO-11-670T (Washington, D.C.: June 23, 2011), and GAO-11-278.

GAO-12-589 FDA's Food Advisory and Recall Process

from USDA's Economic Research Service told us that the risks associated with erroneously ordered recalls or erroneous food-related advisories are not well known. Without data, setting appropriate premiums and policy requirements is difficult.

Loans

If established by Congress, a specific program could be set up by the government to provide or guarantee loans to companies suffering losses from an erroneously ordered food recall or erroneous food-related advisory, and such a program could offer some form of subsidy, according to the relevant literature and our discussions with stakeholders and others. For example, the government could pay a portion of the interest on a loan to a company suffering such losses, provide a grace period before requiring a borrower to begin making interest payments, or charge lower fees than are needed to keep the program self-sustaining. USDA currently offers emergency loans to eligible producers in some instances, such as in a natural disaster. Other federal agencies, such as the Small Business Administration, offer loans with a variety of subsidy levels. Some respondents said an advantage of loans is that producers could receive a loan payment quickly, but some respondents said they would not consider a loan as adequate compensation for a government error. Further, administering loan programs could require additional government resources, such as staff and credit management systems to service loans and monitor default rates.

Nonmonetary Compensation

The government could offer nonmonetary compensation to the food industry, such as a government promotional campaign or a public statement acknowledging an error in recalling a product, according to the relevant literature and our discussions with stakeholders and others. The European Commission used this mechanism with a campaign to promote European fresh produce in response to financial losses stemming from the 2011 outbreak of *E. coli* first associated with cucumbers, lettuce, and tomatoes, then later linked to sprouts grown from fenugreek seeds. Specifically, the European Commission undertook a promotional campaign across all European Union member states to send a message to consumers that European produce was safe and healthful to consume. The campaign used print and audiovisual media to send the message to consumers that cucumbers, tomatoes, and other produce were not connected with the *E. coli* crisis and that European Union food safety standards were strong. Regarding promotional campaigns, some respondents said that their relatively low cost was an advantage, while some said that such campaigns may not be effective. Further, some respondents stated that consumers could be confused if the government warns them not to eat a certain food and then later begins a campaign promoting that food. A few respondents also said the government should be careful not to promote a specific food or industry.

Several Factors May Influence the Development of New Compensation Mechanisms

Several factors highlighted by stakeholders and others may come into play when deciding to establish a new compensation mechanism for the food industry.

Defining What Constitutes an Error

Defining what constitutes an erroneously ordered recall or erroneous food-related advisory and identifying the portion of harm for which the government is responsible may be difficult and specific to each case, in part because of the complexity of identifying the food responsible for an outbreak. For example, some respondents stated that it can be difficult to attribute the cause of a foodborne outbreak with as much certainty as the cause in recalls of products like cars or baby cribs. This difficulty arises in part because one of the main tools used for investigating an outbreak is an epidemiological investigation, which involves, among other things, interviewing those infected about the foods they ate and creating hypotheses about what caused the outbreak. CDC officials acknowledged that epidemiology can be a science that requires a high level of experience and judgment in public health decision making. One legal expert representing industry organizations also told us that, in many cases, the scientific evidence may be inconclusive about whether a recall is justified.

In addition, some respondents stated that it could be difficult to show definitively that a recall or advisory was truly erroneous. For example, an epidemiologist we spoke with told us that when FDA issued an advisory in 2006 identifying spinach as the source of an *E. coli* outbreak, the epidemiology was done correctly to identify spinach as the source. The produce industry expressed concern that advisories such as these were too broad. Nevertheless, FDA officials said they issued a broad advisory because they were still unsure of the exact scope of the problem and chose to be cautious in safeguarding public health. In another example, members of the tomato industry expressed concern that CDC and FDA made errors in identifying and announcing tomatoes as the source of the 2008 *Salmonella* outbreak when the source was later determined to be peppers. An article published in the *New England Journal of Medicine* in March 2011, however, states that the initial public advisory warning consumers to avoid certain types of tomatoes was supported by a strong association between illness outbreaks and the consumption of raw tomatoes. The article states that although an epidemiologic association with raw tomatoes was identified early in the investigation, subsequent epidemiologic and laboratory evidence implicated jalapeño and serrano peppers. The article also states that there was a decline in cases shortly after FDA's nationwide tomato advisory, which could be explained if consumer avoidance of raw tomatoes indirectly reduced their exposure to contaminated jalapeño and serrano peppers.

Identifying the Extent of Government's Responsibility

Identifying the extent of the government's responsibility for losses companies suffer from an erroneously ordered food recall or an erroneous food-related advisory may be difficult. Some losses may be directly attributable to federal actions, while others could be largely outside of government control, such as shifts in consumer demand. For example, the 2011 *Listeria* outbreak in cantaloupes shows that forces largely beyond government control—such as a general decrease in demand for cantaloupes despite FDA's targeted advisory on cantaloupes from one producer in Colorado—also affect industry losses during an outbreak. For example, during the 2011 outbreak, some respondents praised FDA for its timely and targeted public advisories. Even so, demand for cantaloupes plummeted, and USDA reported in November 2011 that prices for cantaloupe dropped about 34 percent during the outbreak. In another example, a USDA study of the *E. coli* outbreak in 2006 found that while spinach sales fell, total expenditures for leafy greens remained unchanged, suggesting that producers of other leafy greens benefitted from FDA's advisory against eating fresh spinach.[33] Issues such as these could make determining government's responsibility more difficult.

Mitigating Potential for Unintended Consequences on Public Health

In funding a mechanism to compensate food producers, some respondents stated that unintended consequences to public health could surface. For example, a few respondents said that if a public health agency, such as FDA, was responsible for funding a mechanism to compensate the food industry and the amount of compensation were large, the agency's ability to carry out its other responsibilities might be hampered. In the case of the 2008 *Salmonella* tomato-pepper outbreak, for example, industry representatives reported an estimated loss of around $145 million to tomato growers and shippers in several states.

---

[33]Carlos Arnade et al., "Consumers Response to the 2006 Foodborne Illness Outbreak Linked to Spinach," *Amber Waves*, vol. 8, no. 1 (Washington, D.C.: USDA Economic Research Service, March 2010), accessed September 29, 2011, http://www.ers.usda.gov/amberwaves/march10/features/outbreakspinach.htm.

These respondents stated that, given that this amount was equivalent to a large portion of FDA's food safety budget in 2008, having to pay industry such an amount could overwhelm the budget of a public health agency like FDA.

In addition, according to some respondents, if FDA were overly concerned about providing compensation, it might wait longer to order recalls or provide food-related advisories until it was sure it had targeted the correct adulterant, potentially exacerbating an outbreak's severity or keeping adulterated products on the shelves, both of which could increase the likelihood that more consumers could become ill or even die. Some respondents told us that making FDA responsible for compensating producers might create perverse incentives for the agency to act in ways that could undermine the public health goals of recalls or food-related advisories. In response to this concern, FDA officials told us they aim to make decisions based on the science of public health and not other factors. Some respondents said that one way to mitigate this problem would be to separate compensation mechanisms from the agencies providing public health services.

Determining Eligibility and Losses Depends on Goals and Objectives

The goals and objectives for any new compensation mechanism provide criteria for decisions, including those on which to base eligibility and funding. For example, some respondents raised questions about eligibility, including which companies along the distribution chain might be eligible for any compensation and whether foreign companies would be included. Some respondents also stated that administering a new mechanism would require determinations about which losses might be covered and that a variety of methods—such as measuring the market value of affected foods or, in the case of farmers, tying compensation to lost production—would be used to determine individual payments.

Similarly, one respondent stated that compensation for recalls versus compensation for advisories could be very different in terms of the number of companies affected, as well as the total overall costs. For example, ordered recalls would be targeted and specific: FDA would not order a generic recall for an entire commodity; rather, the agency would target a lot number or a particular type of product. In such a case, the companies involved would be well known. On the other hand, a food-related advisory can be broader and include a larger group of industry participants throughout the distribution chain. Compensation for an erroneous food-related advisory could require more emphasis on eligibility requirements and criteria for determining which parties would be compensated.

Conclusions

FSMA gave FDA a new tool to use in ensuring the safety of the many foods the agency oversees: the authority to order companies to recall foods other than infant formula that it determines to be adulterated and unsafe. To implement this authority, FDA officials have drafted their internal interim procedures for ordering recalls. It remains unclear, however, how effective the agency will be in fully implementing this new authority. First, FDA has not made public procedures for ordering food recalls. Specifically, (1) FDA's internal procedures have not been made public, and (2) the agency has not issued regulations or industry guidance publicly clarifying its procedures for ordering food recalls—including how the agency will weigh evidence on whether a recall is necessary—and FDA officials told us the agency had not decided whether to provide such information. Without this information, the agency cannot ensure that it applies practices uniformly or consistently or that it gives clear information to the food industry or to consumers and the public. Second, FDA's data on ordered recalls of nonfood products appear to be unreliable. As it relates to this data, (1) the categories for ordered recalls in its central database have undocumented definitions and (2) the databases that contain recall data do not fully share information. Given these issues, it is not clear whether or to what extent the agency's data on ordered food recalls can be relied upon to report accurate information to Congress and the public. Third, FDA faces challenges in how it communicates information about food recalls and outbreaks of foodborne illnesses. FDA has taken several steps to begin meeting these challenges, but the agency has not adopted a recommendation from its risk communication committee to develop a policy for communications during emerging events or from the Institute of Medicine and National Research Council to develop, in conjunction with other federal agencies, a coordinated plan for crisis communications. As a result, FDA is not clarifying for those outside the agency what to expect from FDA communications, and the agency continues to risk providing information on foodborne illnesses that conflicts with the information provided by other agencies or confuses consumers. In addition, FDA has not fully adopted a recommendation from our prior report to work jointly with USDA to identify any additional approaches needed to advise consumers about recalls,[34] despite input from others to consider new approaches and a related change in USDA policy concerning public notifications. We continue to believe that in not implementing this recommendation, FDA is missing opportunities to learn

---

[34]GAO-05-51.

from USDA's experiences and strengthen its food recall and advisory procedures.

| Recommendations for Executive Action | We recommend that the Secretary of Health and Human Services direct the Commissioner of FDA to take the following seven actions:

To strengthen FDA's process for ordering recalls,

- document FDA's process for ordering food recalls in publicly available procedures;

- document FDA's process for ordering food recalls in regulations or industry guidance to include information on how the agency will weigh evidence on whether a recall is necessary;

- document definitions for categories of ordered recalls in the agency's central recall database; and

- identify and implement ways to improve information sharing among its databases that contain recall data.

To address FDA's communication challenges in advising the public about food recalls and outbreaks, implement recommendations:

- from FDA's risk communication committee to develop a policy for communications during emerging events;

- from the Institute of Medicine and National Research Council to develop, in conjunction with other federal agencies, a coordinated plan for crisis communications; and

- following from our prior work and others' input to consult with USDA on lessons learned in advising consumers about recalls to determine whether any of USDA's practices may be feasible at FDA, as consistent with applicable law.

Agency Comments and our Evaluation

We provided a copy of our draft report to the Department of Health and Human Services for their review and comment. We also provided a draft of this report as a courtesy to the Consumer Product Safety Commission, Environmental Protection Agency, the Department of Transportation's National Highway Traffic Safety Administration, the Department of State, and USDA. On July 9, 2012, we received written comments from HHS, which are reproduced in appendix IV. HHS neither agreed nor disagreed with the recommendations in the report, but stated that HHS and FDA will explore each recommendation as they consider how to implement the recall provisions of FSMA. HHS also provided information on actions in process that are to address most of the recommendations we made in our draft report. The additional information related to each of our seven recommendations follows:

- *Document FDA's process for ordering food recalls in publicly available procedures:* HHS stated that FDA is in the process of incorporating these procedures formally into its Regulatory Procedures Manual (a publicly available document), and expects the procedures for recalls of ordered food to be available in that manual by fall 2012.

- *Document FDA's process for ordering food recalls in regulations or industry guidance to include information on how the agency will weigh evidence on whether a recall is necessary:* HHS stated that FDA agrees on the importance of providing information to stakeholders on how the agency will weigh evidence on whether a recall is necessary and has convened workgroups that are actively considering options for providing information to stakeholders.

- *Document definitions for categories of ordered recalls in the agency's central recall database:* HHS stated that FDA has begun work to update the agency's central recall database and is updating its data to more adequately reflect the different types of recalls documented in that system. HHS stated that FDA expects to complete these changes by fall 2012.

- *Identify and implement ways to improve information sharing among its databases that contain recall data:* HHS stated that FDA maintains the central recall database as its primary system for documenting and managing recalls of all FDA-regulated products, and that FDA's Office of Information Management manages information technology to ensure FDA has a robust information technology foundation enabling interoperability across FDA and the development of systems necessary to meet FDA's mission.

- *Implement recommendations from FDA's risk communication committee to develop a policy for communications during emerging events:* HHS stated that FDA is exploring the feasibility and objectives of a policy for communications during emerging events.

- *Implement a recommendation from the Institute of Medicine and National Research Council to develop, in conjunction with other federal agencies, a coordinated plan for crisis communications:* HHS stated that FDA's work with the Department of Homeland Security's National Incident Management System will address this recommendation and will provide for a consistent nationwide approach for federal, state, local, and tribal governments to work effectively and efficiently together to prepare for, prevent, respond to, and recover from domestic incidents.

- *Implement recommendations following from our prior work and others' input to consult with USDA on lessons learned in advising consumers about recalls to determine whether any of USDA's practices may be feasible at FDA, as consistent with applicable law:* HHS stated that FDA will continue to work with USDA to gain insight and determine whether any of USDA's current practices may be feasible at FDA.

The actions HHS describes, if appropriately implemented, could help to address most of the recommendations we made. However, HHS did not provide information on actions related to our recommendation that it identify and implement ways to improve information sharing among its databases that contain recall data. We continue to believe that improved information sharing among these databases could help to ensure the data are consistent and accurate. HHS also provided technical comments, which we incorporated as appropriate.

We are sending copies of this report to the Secretaries of Health and Human Services, Agriculture, and State; the Administrators of the Environmental Protection Agency and the Department of Transportation's National Highway Traffic Safety Administration; the Chairman of the Consumer Product Safety Commission; appropriate congressional committees; and other interested parties. In addition, the report is available at no charge on the GAO website at http://www.gao.gov.

If you or your staff members have any questions about this report, please contact me at (202) 512-3841 or shamesl@gao.gov. Contact points for our Offices of Congressional Relations and Public Affairs may be found on the last page of this report. GAO staff who made key contributions to this report are listed in appendix V.

Lisa Shames
Director, Natural Resources and Environment

List of Committees

The Honorable Debbie Stabenow
Chairwoman
The Honorable Pat Roberts
Ranking Member
Committee on Agriculture, Nutrition, and Forestry
United States Senate

The Honorable Tom Harkin
Chairman
The Honorable Michael Enzi
Ranking Member
Committee on Health, Education, Labor, and Pensions
United States Senate

The Honorable Frank Lucas
Chairman
The Honorable Collin Peterson
Ranking Member
Committee on Agriculture
House of Representatives

The Honorable Fred Upton
Chairman
The Honorable Henry Waxman
Ranking Member
Committee on Energy and Commerce
House of Representatives

Appendix I: Objectives, Scope, and Methodology

This report (1) examines key government entities having the authority to order product recalls and how the Food and Drug Administration (FDA) implements its authority; (2) examines the challenges FDA faces, if any, in advising the public about food recalls or outbreaks of foodborne illnesses and examines how FDA has addressed these challenges; and (3) identifies mechanisms that may compensate the food industry for erroneously ordered food recalls or erroneous food-related advisories, including the advantages and disadvantages of each.[1]

To address all our objectives, we reviewed information from the Congressional Research Service, the National Academies, and our own past work, as well as from academic sources and industry publications. We also gathered documentation and met with officials from FDA, the Centers for Disease Control and Prevention (CDC), the Consumer Product Safety Commission, the Environmental Protection Agency, the Department of Transportation's National Highway Traffic Safety Administration, the Department of State, and the Department of Agriculture (USDA), as well as with representatives of the food industry, consumer groups, and others to understand the broader issues surrounding recalls and FDA's food-related advisories.

To address our first objective, we first determined key state, federal, and international government entities with authority to order recalls. To identify key state agencies, we used help from the Association of Food and Drug Officials to send an e-mail to its members inquiring about their authority to order recalls. A total of 16 states and Puerto Rico responded to the association's inquiry. We followed up with officials from those states and territory to clarify their authorities and collect supporting documentation, such as state statutes and regulations, and through this process, we identified those with the authority to order food recalls. To identify key federal agencies, we reviewed our prior work in this area, collected legal documentation, and interviewed officials from FDA, the Consumer Product Safety Commission, the Environmental Protection Agency, the National Highway Traffic Safety Administration, and USDA. To identify

---

[1]For purposes of this report, the term *recall* includes a firm's removal or correction of a marketed product. Corrections may include repair, modification, adjustment, relabeling, destruction, or inspection of a product without its physical removal to some other location. Similarly, the term *order* includes an agency's authority to directly mandate, require, or make a determination that would require a recall under the law, or an agency's authority to obtain such an order through a court.

international government entities with the authority to order food recalls, we reviewed a 2010 report from the National Academies on FDA's oversight of food safety, as well as our prior work in this area. We also interviewed officials from Australia, Canada, the European Union, and New Zealand. To determine how FDA implements its authority to order food recalls (other than infant formula), we reviewed the FDA Food Safety Modernization Act (FSMA) and internal interim procedures on food recalls as provided by FDA officials. The information presented in appendix II of this report on the steps FDA takes to order food recalls (other than infant formula) is based on statute. To compare how FDA implements its authority for food with how FDA and other agencies implement their authority for other products, we reviewed relevant documents obtained from key federal agencies, as well as some countries such as Canada. Key documents we reviewed included statutes; regulations; guidance to industry such as the Consumer Product Safety Commission's *Regulated Products Handbook*;[2] and internal guidance for staff. This internal guidance included FDA's *Regulatory Procedures Manual*;[3] the National Highway Traffic Safety Administration's *Office Procedures for Conducting Defect Investigations*;[4] and the Environmental Protection Agency's *Federal Insecticide, Fungicide, and Rodenticide Act Inspection Manual*.[5] We also collected information on the number of ordered recalls from fiscal year 2006 through fiscal year 2010 from FDA, the Consumer Product Safety Commission, the Environmental Protection Agency, and the National Highway Traffic Safety Administration. We requested from FDA the number of ordered recalls in the agency's history. FDA officials reported that the data they provided us came from the agency's current database for recall information, known as the Recall Enterprise System. We determined that these data were not reliable for our reporting purposes. A larger discussion of these issues is contained our first objective.

---

[2]U.S. Consumer Product Safety Commission. *Regulated Products Handbook* (Washington, D.C.: 2005).

[3]U.S. Department of Health and Human Services, Food and Drug Administration, *Regulatory Procedures Manual*. (Silver Spring, MD: 2011).

[4]U.S. Department of Transportation, National Highway Traffic Safety Administration, *Office Procedures for Conducting Defect Investigations* (Washington, D.C.: 2009).

[5]U. S. Environmental Protection Agency, Office of Enforcement and Compliance Assurance, *Federal Insecticide, Fungicide, and Rodenticide Act (FIFRA) Inspection Manual* (Washington, D.C.: 2002).

To address our second objective, we first identified challenges FDA may
face in advising the public about food recalls or outbreaks of foodborne
illnesses by reviewing the following reports: FDA's *Strategic Plan for Risk
Communication*[6] and FDA's *Communicating Risks and Benefits: An
Evidence-Based User's Guide*;[7] the Institute of Medicine and National
Research Council's 2010 report, *Enhancing Food Safety: The Role of the
Food and Drug Administration*;[8] and *Stronger Partnerships for Safer
Food: An Agenda for Strengthening State and Local Roles in the Nation's
Food Safety System*.[9] We also reviewed documents from relevant
meetings of FDA's Advisory Committee on Risk Communication (risk
communication committee) and our prior work. We verified the challenges
we identified during meetings with FDA officials, representatives from the
food industry and consumer organizations, state and federal government
officials, and experts in food safety. To determine the steps FDA is taking
to address these challenges, we used three methods. First, we compared
the challenges we identified with our analysis of FDA's *Strategic Plan for
Risk Communication*, the Institute of Medicine and National Research
Council's 2010 report on FDA's food safety role, transcripts from
meetings of FDA's risk communication committee, other relevant agency
documents, and our prior work. Second, we interviewed consumer and
industry stakeholders, government officials, and experts in food safety or
food law for their perspectives on FDA's actions to address these
challenges. And third, we interviewed FDA officials about their efforts to
address each challenge.

To address our third objective, we first gathered information on what
mechanisms might be used by meeting with representatives of consumer
and industry organizations, experts in food safety and food law, and
officials from state and other federal agencies. We also reviewed the

---

[6]U.S. Department of Health and Human Services, Food and Drug Administration,
Strategic Plan for Risk Communication (Silver Spring, MD: Fall 2009).

[7]U.S. Department of Health and Human Services, Food and Drug Administration,
Communicating Risks and Benefits: An Evidence-Based Use's Guide (Silver Spring, MD:
August 2011).

[8]Robert B. Wallace and Maria Oria, eds., *Enhancing Food Safety: The Role of the Food
and Drug Administration* (Washington, D.C.: National Academies Press, 2010).

[9]Michael R. Taylor and Stephanie D. David, *Stronger Partnerships for Safer Food: An
Agenda for Strengthening State and Local Roles in the Nation's Food Safety System*
(Washington, D.C.: George Washington University School of Public Health and Health
Services, April 2009).

relevant literature, including *The Tools of Government: A Guide to the New Governance*,[10] an authoritative work about government policy tools. In addition, we collected documentation and interviewed officials from international government entities including Australia, Canada, the European Union, and New Zealand about their knowledge of possible compensation mechanisms.

To gather information on the advantages and disadvantages of possible mechanisms, we conducted semistructured interviews with 16 individuals having expertise or a stake in this topic and analyzed their responses. We chose the 16 to reflect a range of perspectives. Specifically, we interviewed 5 representatives each from consumer and industry organizations, 3 officials from federal or state government, and 3 experts in food safety or food law. To develop and execute these interviews, we first developed draft interview questions and a script to follow to ensure that interviewers asked the same questions in the same manner in every interview. We also conducted two pretests of the interview questions and script and made modifications based on those pretests. In advance of each interview, we provided each respondent with a list of factors to consider and possible mechanisms that we would cover during our interview. We conducted all our semistructured interviews via telephone. To characterize the results of these interviews, we defined the words used to quantify the results as follows: "one" means one respondent, "a few" means two or three respondents, "some" means four or five respondents, and "almost half" means six or seven respondents. We gathered stakeholders' perspectives on each mechanism but did not independently evaluate the viability of any mechanism, its advantages, or disadvantages.

We conducted this performance audit from May 2011 to July 2012 in accordance with generally accepted government auditing standards. Those standards require that we plan and perform the audit to obtain sufficient, appropriate evidence to provide a reasonable basis for our findings and conclusions based on our audit objectives. We believe that the evidence obtained provides a reasonable basis for our findings and conclusions based on our audit objectives.

---

[10]Lester Salamon, ed., *The Tools of Government: A Guide to the New Governance* (New York: Oxford University Press, 2002).

Appendix II: Processes for Ordering Product Recalls at Key Federal Agencies

Four key federal agencies have the authority to recall products they regulate, and each agency's process for ordering a recall conforms with provisions in statutes, regulations, and procedures, as summarized in table 2. While companies can voluntarily recall their products at any time, the table below specifies points in the ordered recall process when agencies generally offer companies the opportunity to voluntarily issue a recall.

Table 2: Steps Key Federal Agencies Take When Ordering Product Recalls

Agency	Product	Steps
Food and Drug Administration	Foods	1. The agency determines there is a reasonable probability that a food, other than infant formula, is adulterated under the Federal Food, Drug, and Cosmetic Act, or misbranded with respect to labeling for a major food allergen and that use of or exposure to the food will cause serious health consequences or death to humans or animals.
		2. Company is provided with an opportunity to voluntarily cease distribution of the food and recall it.
		3. If company does not take voluntary action, FDA may order company to cease distribution and notify all others along the supply chain to cease distribution.
		4. FDA provides the company an opportunity for informal hearing before the agency.
		5. If FDA determines that removal of the product is necessary then the agency shall, as appropriate, amend the cease-distribution order to require recall of the product.
	Infant formula	1. Agency determines that formula processed by the manufacturer presents a risk to human health.
		2. The manufacturer must immediately recall the product and report on actions taken to implement the recall.[a]
		3. The Federal Food, Drug, and Cosmetic Act prohibits the failure to provide such reports to FDA or take certain actions, as directed by FDA in regulation, to inform the public of the recall.
	Medical devices	1. Agency determines there is a reasonable probability that a medical device would cause serious adverse health consequences or death.
		2. Company may, under FDA policy, voluntarily recall the product.[a]
		3. If company does not voluntarily recall the product, the agency may order the company to immediately cease distribution and notify health professionals and device user facilities of the order and instruct them to stop using the device.
		4. Company has an opportunity for an informal hearing before the FDA Commissioner.
		5. Agency may amend the cease-distribution order to require a recall of the product.

Agency	Product	Steps
	Radiation-emitting electronic products	1. FDA determines a product contains a defect relating to safety of use by reason of emission of electronic radiation or does not comply with applicable standards.
		2. Agency notifies the company of defect or failure to comply with standards.
		3. Company may, under FDA policy, voluntarily recall the product.[a]
		4. The company is given an opportunity to respond to FDA and present its views and evidence before the agency.
		5. Following a hearing, if FDA maintains that the product has a defect relating to safety of use by reason of emission or electronic radiation or does not comply with applicable standards, the agency will direct the company to provide notification of defect or failure to comply with standards.
		6. The company must bring the product into conformity, replace the product, or refund the cost.[b]
	Licensed biological products	1. Agency determines a product presents an imminent or substantial hazard to the public health.
		2. FDA issues an immediate recall.
		3. Company is afforded an opportunity for a formal hearing.
	Tobacco products	1. Agency determines that there is a reasonable probability that a tobacco product contains a manufacturing defect not ordinarily contained in tobacco products on the market that would cause serious, adverse health consequences or death.
		2. Company may, under FDA policy, voluntarily recall the product.[a]
		3. If the company does not voluntarily recall the product, the agency orders company to cease distribution of the product.
		4. Company is provided with an opportunity for an informal hearing.
		5. Agency may amend the cease-distribution order to require recall of the product.
Consumer Product Safety Commission	Consumer goods: products presenting a substantial hazard[c]	1. Agency determines that a product does not comply with applicable consumer product safety rules or any other rule, regulation, standard, or ban under the Consumer Product Safety Act or any other statute enforced by the commission or contains a defect that could create a substantial product hazard or creates an unreasonable risk of serious injury or death.
		2. Agency notifies company of its analysis and determination and orders the company to cease distribution and provide notification.
		3. Agency offers company an opportunity to take voluntary action and correct the violation. Company may request an informal hearing and present information contrary to commission's determination.
		4. Agency may order the company to repair, replace, or refund the product.
	Consumer goods: products presenting an imminent hazard[d]	1. Agency determines that a product presents imminent and unreasonable risk of death, serious illness, or severe personal injury.
		2. Agency files an action in U.S. District Court for court approval for a recall order.

Agency	Product	Steps
Environmental Protection Agency	Vehicles and engines	1. Agency determines that a substantial number of a class or category of vehicles or engines do not conform to emission standards as specified in regulations.
		2. Agency notifies company of noncompliance and requires company to submit a plan to remedy the nonconformity.
		3. Company has opportunity to submit a plan for a recall and may implement voluntary recall.
		4. Company is provided an opportunity for a public hearing.
		5. Agency requires company to remedy the nonconformity.
	Pesticides	1. Agency determines a pesticide does not comply with statutory requirements or causes unreasonable adverse effects on human health or the environment.
		2. Agency notifies the registrant and the public of the intent to cancel or to hold a hearing on whether or not to cancel a pesticide's registration.
		3. If agency determines the pesticide causes an imminent hazard, it will suspend the registration, pending the completion of the cancellation process.
		4. Company is offered an expedited hearing on whether an imminent hazard exists.
		5. Agency determines that a pesticide with a registration that has been suspended and canceled should be recalled to protect health or the environment.
		6. If agency determines a voluntary recall may be safe or effective, it may request a recall plan from the company.
		7. If agency approves the voluntary recall plan, the company can implement the voluntarily recall plan.
		8. If agency finds a mandatory plan is necessary or that the requested recall plan is inadequate, it shall issue a regulation that prescribes a plan for recalling the pesticide.
National Highway Traffic Safety Administration	Motor vehicles, replacement equipment	1. Agency makes an initial determination that a safety-related defect exists or that a product does not comply with an applicable federal motor vehicle safety standard.
		2. Agency gives manufacturer an opportunity to present information. This may be by way of a public meeting, hearing, or submission of written comments.
		3. Manufacturer may voluntarily recall the product.
		4. If the company does not voluntarily recall the product, the agency may make a final decision that a safety-related defect exists or that a product does not comply with an applicable federal motor vehicle safety standard.
		5. If agency still determines recall is warranted, it may order the company to provide notice and recall the product.

Sources: GAO analysis of statutes, regulations, and procedures.

[a]FDA's *Regulatory Procedures Manual* states that firms may initiate a recall at any time, such as following notification of a problem by FDA or a state agency, to fulfill their responsbility to protect public health from products presenting a risk of injury or gross deception that are otherwise defective.

[b]For purposes of this report, the term *recall* includes a firm's removal or correction of a marketed product. *Corrections* may include repair, modification, adjustment, relabeling, destruction, or inspection of a product without its physical removal to some other location.

[c]A substantial product hazard is defined as (1) a failure to comply with an applicable consumer product safety rule, regulation, standard or ban under any other act enforced by the Consumer Product Safety Commission which creates a substantial risk of injury to the public or (2) a product defect which creates a substantial risk of injury to the public.

[d]An imminently hazardous consumer product means a consumer product that presents imminent and unreasonable risk of death, serious illness, or severe personal injury.

Appendix III: FDA Data Related to Ordered Recalls

We noted a number of inconsistencies in FDA's data on ordered recalls during our analysis, which are described in table 3.

Table 3: Problems with FDA Data Related to Ordered Recalls

Recall Enterprise System recall event identification number	Fiscal year	Product	Problem
25991	2002	Biological product	Center for Biologics Evaluation and Research officials told us that there were two ordered recalls of biological products in fiscal year 2006. Officials from the Office of Regulatory Affairs provided data from the Recall Enterprise System also indicating two ordered recalls in the agency's history but not occurring in fiscal year 2006. Officials from the Center for Biologics Evaluation and Research later stated that, after further investigation, they realized the two presumed ordered recalls from fiscal year 2006 were actually orders to cease manufacturing, not orders to recall. When asked about this new information, Office of Regulatory Affairs officials reexamined Recall Enterprise System data and acknowledged they erroneously told us there were two ordered recalls for fiscal year 2006; the officials confirmed that these two events were orders to cease manufacturing, not orders to recall. Officials also told us that one ordered recall had occurred, in 2002.
26205	2003	Medical device	Center for Devices and Radiological Health officials provided data indicating ordered recalls of medical devices had occurred but the Recall Enterprise System data indicated that the recalls were ordered under regulations governing the recall of human tissue intended for transplantation, which are biological products, not medical devices.
26286	2003		
34692	2006	Not provided	Following its original data submission to GAO, Center for Devices and Radiological Health officials provided data indicating three additional ordered recalls of a product regulated by the center occurred in fiscal years 2006 and 2010. Agency officials told us these three recalls were not FDA-ordered recalls but voluntary recalls initiated by FDA. In the Recall Enterprise System, FDA requested recalls are inaccurately categorized as ordered recalls.
55825	2010	Not provided	
56162	2010	Not provided	
27549	2004	Radiation-emitting electronic product	Center for Devices and Radiological health officials provided data indicating that this recall was ordered, but an internal memo stated that this recall would be classified as a voluntary recall.
38233	2007	Radiation-emitting electronic product	These recalls were reflected in data reported by Center for Devices and Radiological Health officials but not included in data reported by Office of Regulatory Affairs officials. Officials from both said their data came from the Recall Enterprise System.
38248	2007		
56425	2011	Medical device	A notice posted on FDA's website indicates that the agency ordered this recall; Center for Devices and Radiological Health officials provided data from the Recall Enterprise System indicating this recall was court ordered.
			Center for Devices and Radiological Health officials provided data from the Recall Enterprise System indicating that this recall occurred in fiscal year 2010. Office of Regulatory Affairs officials said the date in the Recall Enterprise System was incorrect and that the recall occurred in fiscal year 2011.

Source: GAO analysis of FDA data.

Appendix IV: Comments from the Department of Health and Human Services

DEPARTMENT OF HEALTH & HUMAN SERVICES   OFFICE OF THE SECRETARY

Assistant Secretary for Legislation
Washington, DC 20201

JUL 9 2012

Lisa Shames
Director, Natural Resources and Environment
U.S. Government Accountability Office
441 G Street NW
Washington, DC 20548

Dear Ms. Shames:

Attached are comments on the U.S. Government Accountability Office's (GAO) report entitled,
"Food Safety: FDA's Food Advisory and Recall Process Needs Strengthening" (GAO-12-589).

The Department appreciates the opportunity to review this report prior to publication.

Sincerely,

Jim R. Esquea
Assistant Secretary for Legislation

Attachment

GENERAL COMMENTS OF THE DEPARTMENT OF HEALTH AND HUMAN SERVICES (HHS) ON THE GOVERNMENT ACCOUNTABILITY OFFICE'S (GAO) DRAFT REPORT ENTITLED, "FOOD SAFETY: FDA'S FOOD ADVISORY AND RECALL PROCESS NEEDS STENGTHENING" (GAO-12-589)

The Department appreciates the opportunity to comment on this draft report. HHS and FDA will explore each recommendation fully as we consider how to implement the recall provisions of the FDA Food Safety Modernization Act (FSMA). FDA has already put processes and systems in place that will address many of GAO's recommendations.

Food recalls are complex and multi-faceted, and they require expeditious yet thorough action by industry, FDA, and its federal and state partners in an effort that combines science and corrective action. A precedent for many recalls, whether voluntary or mandatory, is a rigorous epidemiological investigation that requires the cooperation of the states, the Centers for Disease Control and Prevention (CDC), and FDA.

FSMA gives FDA, CDC, and other federal agencies new responsibilities to enhance federal, state, and local surveillance systems for foodborne illness so that they can identify and control outbreaks more rapidly. While FSMA gives FDA the authority to order that certain adulterated or misbranded foods are promptly removed from commerce, FSMA also provides a framework for heightened multi-agency involvement that will strengthen FDA in its recall efforts.

GAO Recommendations:

1. That FDA document its process for ordering food recalls in publicly available procedures.

FDA has completed an interim Standard Operating Procedure (SOP) that outlines the steps for ordering food recalls. FDA is currently in the process of incorporating these SOPs formally into the Regulatory Procedures Manual (RPM). FDA anticipates that the procedure for ordered recalls of foods will be available in the RPM by Fall 2012.

2. That FDA establish regulations or industry guidance (or both) for ordering food recalls.

FDA agrees that it is important to provide information to stakeholders on how the Agency will weigh evidence on whether a recall is necessary and has convened workgroups that are actively considering options for providing information to stakeholders.

3. That FDA develop definitions for categories of ordered recalls in the agency's central recall database.

FDA has begun work to update the Agency's central recall database known as the Recall Enterprise System (RES). FDA is also in the process of updating the data set of recalls in RES to more adequately reflect the different types of recalls that are documented in the system, i.e., voluntary recalls and other recalls that are undertaken under FDA's recall authorities. FDA expects to complete the changes to RES by Fall 2012.

1

**GENERAL COMMENTS OF THE DEPARTMENT OF HEALTH AND HUMAN
SERVICES (HHS) ON THE GOVERNMENT ACCOUNTABILITY OFFICE'S (GAO)
DRAFT REPORT ENTITLED, "FOOD SAFETY: FDA'S FOOD ADVISORY AND
RECALL PROCESS NEEDS STENGTHENING" (GAO-12-589)**

*4. That FDA identify and implement ways to improve information sharing among its databases
that contain food recall data.*

FDA maintains the RES as the primary enterprise-wide system for documenting and managing
recalls of all FDA-regulated products. FDA's Office of Information Management manages
information technology (IT) and other related services including technical oversight of system
development processes, policies, and methodologies and management of IT infrastructure to
ensure FDA has a robust IT foundation that enables interoperability across FDA and allows
development of systems necessary to meet FDA's mission of promoting and protecting public
health in an efficient, effective, productive, and timely manner.

*5. That FDA implement recommendation from FDA's Risk Advisory Committee to develop a
policy for communications during emerging events.*

FDA is exploring the feasibility and objectives of a policy for communications during emerging
events. FDA has developed a new format for news releases that addresses issues mentioned by
the committee. FDA first used this new format in the Spring 2010. FDA also established a
procedure for expediting the clearance of outbreak-related press releases by establishing a
maximum 6-hour timeline from the start of the review of the draft of a public health
emergency/outbreak-related press release to its dissemination to the media.

The Interagency Foodborne Outbreak Response Working Group, with membership from FDA,
CDC, and the United States Department of Agriculture (USDA), is working to improve federal
interagency collaboration and communication during multistate foodborne illness outbreak
investigations and response. Projects include: (1) evaluating interagency communication after
interagency outbreak response, (2) developing procedures for rapid coordination and clearance of
public information products during outbreaks, and (3) developing templates and Standard
Operating Procedures for public communications related to outbreaks and how to communicate
uncertainty and changes in messaging as new information becomes available.

*6. That FDA implement a recommendation from the IOM and National Research Council to
develop, in conjunction with other federal agencies, a coordinated plan for crisis
communications.*

FDA's work with the National Incident Management System (NIMS), developed and
administered by the Department of Homeland Security, will address this recommendation.
NIMS will provide for a consistent nationwide approach for federal, state, local, and tribal
governments to work effectively and efficiently together to prepare for, prevent, respond to, and
recover from domestic incidents, regardless of cause, size, or complexity.

NIMS enhances the management of domestic incidents by establishing a single, comprehensive
system for incident management and helps to achieve greater cooperation among agencies at all

2

**GENERAL COMMENTS OF THE DEPARTMENT OF HEALTH AND HUMAN
SERVICES (HHS) ON THE GOVERNMENT ACCOUNTABILITY OFFICE'S (GAO)
DRAFT REPORT ENTITLED, "FOOD SAFETY: FDA'S FOOD ADVISORY AND
RECALL PROCESS NEEDS STENGTHENING" (GAO-12-589)**

levels of government. Implementing the NIMS strengthens each agency's capability and resolve
to fulfill its responsibilities to the public during emergencies.

*7. That FDA implement a recommendation from GAO's prior work and other's input to consult
with USDA on lessons learned in advising consumers about recalls to determine whether any of
USDA's practices may be feasible at FDA, as consistent with applicable law.*

FDA will continue to work closely with USDA's Food Safety and Inspection Service to gain
insight and determine whether any of USDA's current practices may be feasible at FDA.

3

Appendix V: GAO Contact and Staff Acknowledgments

GAO Contact	Lisa Shames, (202) 512-3841 or shamesl@gao.gov
Staff Acknowledgments	In addition to the individual named above, Karen Jones (Assistant Director), Kevin Bray, Mark Braza, Candace Carpenter, Ellen W. Chu, Barbara El Osta, Brendan Kretzschmar, Kirsten B. Lauber, Angela Miles, and Kiki Theodoropolous made key contributions to this report.

www.ingramcontent.com/pod-product-compliance
Lightning Source LLC
Chambersburg PA
CBHW082244310526
45795CB00014B/2414